Nigel Cawthorne is the author of 164 books under his own name and as Al Cimino, Alexander Macdonald and Gordon Power. He is thought to be the most published living author in the UK. He was called to testify to the US Senate over *The Bamboo Cage*. *The Iron Cage* prompted questions in both houses of the British parliament. *Sex Lives of the US Presidents* got him on the *Joan Rivers Show* and *Sex Lives of the Popes* got him on the biggest chat show in Brazil. He lives in Bloomsbury, London, just a few minutes walk from the British Library.

D1589482

Other books by Nigel Cawthorne

*The Empress of South America – The Irish Courtesan Who Destroyed Paraguay and
    Became Its National Heroine*
Flight MH370 – The Mystery
The Bamboo Cage – The True Story of American POWs in Vietnam
The Iron Cage – Are British POWs Still Alive in Siberia?
Daughter of Heaven – The True Story of the Only Woman to Become Emperor of China
Takin' Back My Name – The Confessions of Ike Turner
Reaping the Whirlwind – Voices of the Enemy from World War II
Sex Lives of the Popes
Sex Lives of the US Presidents
Sex Lives of the Great Dictators
Sex Lives of the Kings and Queens of England
Sex Lives of the Hollywood Goddesses
Sex Lives of the Hollywood Idols
Sex Lives of the Great Artists
Sex Lives of the Great Composers
Sex Lives of the Hollywood Goddesses 2
Sex Lives of the Famous Gays
Sex Lives of the Famous Lesbians
Sex Lives of the Roman Emperors
Strange Laws of Old England
Curious Cures of Old England
Amorous Antics of Old England
Sex Secrets of Old England
Beastly Battles of Old England
Flight MH370: The Mystery
Vietnam: A War Lost and Won
House of Horrors: The True Story of Josef Fritzl, The Father from Hell
Jack the Ripper's Secret Confession
Jeremy Clarkson: Motormouth
Magical Mythtery Tour
The History of the SS Cricket Team
The Alien Who Thought He Was Elvis
Che Guevara – The Last Conquistador
Julius Caesar
Alexander the Great
Blond Ambition: The Rise and Rise of Boris Johnson
David Cameron – Class Act
Alan Johnson – Left Standing
Portraits of Power
Ian Fleming: Licence to Kill
Harry – A Prince Among Men
A Bit of Stephen Fry

JEREMY CORBYN
LEADING FROM THE LEFT

NIGEL CAWTHORNE

Table of Contents

Chapter One – Coming from the Left   1

Chapter Two – Apprenticeship in Politics   11

Chapter Three – The Campaign Group   19

Chapter Four – A Thorn in the Side   29

Chapter Five – Friends on the Left   43

Chapter Six – Swimming Against the Tide   55

Chapter Seven – Not New Labour   65

Chapter Eight – A Matter of Principle   79

Chapter Nine – The Brown Years   91

Chapter Ten – Return to the Wilderness   97

Chapter Eleven – Jez We Can   111

Chapter Twelve – The PLP versus the Party   117

Chapter One – Coming from the Left

This is the first biography of veteran left-winger Jeremy Corbyn, perhaps because, like his mentor and long-time friend Tony Benn, he believes that politics is about policy, not personality. Shortly after securing the nomination to enter the Labour leadership race, Corbyn told the media: "I don't do personal, I'm more interested in ideas and politics."

With his beard and his raft of radical opinions, it was easy to paint him as an anachronism, the sort of old-fashioned lefty thought to have died out in the 1950s, if not the 1930s. However, even Boris Johnson has praised him for his authenticity. In a Labour Party full of "relatively anaemic, gelatinous and vacillating opportunists – Jeremy Corbyn looks passionate and principled," said the Mayor of London.

Like Tony Benn, Michael Foot, Lenin, Che Guevara and even Karl Marx himself, Corbyn is not a product of the working classes. He is a socialist out of commitment and conscience. His father David Corbyn was an electrical engineer and his mother Naomi was a maths teacher for a girls' grammar school. However, they were politically committed and met on a committee which called for the end of the Spanish Civil War.

"Mum and Dad met campaigning on the Spanish civil war," said Corbyn. "Both were active peace campaigners. They died in 1986 and '87. Dad would be a hundred now."

True to the cause, rather than returning to the family home when his mother was on her deathbed, Corbyn was at a left-wing political meeting in the Midlands with his brother Piers. Piers later said that they thought "Mum would have said 'just get on with it,' so that's what he did."

Jeremy Bernard Corbyn was the youngest of four brothers. The others all went on to become scientists. He was born on 26 May 1949 in Chippenham, Wiltshire, a market town in the southern Cotswolds, and was brought up in rural Shropshire. As a boy, he liked working on local farms. Even in his north Islington constituency, he maintained links with his rustic upbringing, growing fruit and vegetables on his allotment in East Finchley.

He had been on the waiting list for years before a plot finally came up in March 2003 – the week the Iraq war broke out. Although he was busy protesting against the US-led invasion, he took it on the plot anyway, burning down derelict sheds that were there and planted growing potatoes, beans, soft fruit and apples:

"I try to grow things that don't require a lot of watering because I don't get up there regularly enough," he said. "I always make time for my allotment. You like a dry summer because the weeds don't grow. You water what you need to water and the weeds can sod off."

Chris McKane, chairman of the East Finchley allotment holders' association, said: "He doesn't grow anything fancy – broad beans, sweetcorn and potatoes, all organic. He's a good cultivator, very good with a mattock."

Corbyn has been interested in environmental issues since his youth and believes in giving communities greater powers to local energy schemes, as they do in Germany, and he calls for "houses with gardens for everyone", adding that "anyone who wants to be a beekeeper should be a beekeeper".

He acknowledged there would be problems in giving everyone a taste of the rural idyll he was brought up in:

"To give everyone a house and garden is very difficult in urban areas," he said. "But we can achieve something, and I've been involved with converting ground-floor car-parking spaces to growing areas on council estates in my area, giving people access to small growing areas. Children growing potatoes and tomatoes in their own soil is something they never forget."

At home, he and his brother were encouraged to discuss current affairs and Jeremy was given a book of George Orwell's essays as a present at the age of sixteen. Both he and Piers joined the local Wrekin Labour and Young Socialists party.

"They were all politically engaged," Jane Chapman who, as Jeremy's first wife. got to know the family later. " There was always a lot of political discussion round the dinner table. His parents belonged to the local Labour Party. So from quite an early age, he was politicized."

Piers was further to the left than his younger brother. He later joined the Communist Party and a member of the revolutionary

International Marxist Group before joining the Bermondsey Labour Party, whose candidate was then gay-rights activist Peter Tatchell.

But while Jeremy was solely interest in politics from an early age, Piers developed other interests. Fascinated with the weather and climate patterns, he began constructing his own observation equipment at the age of five. Showing the same single-minded dedication as his brother, Piers studied physics at Imperial College. Graduating with first-class honours, he went on to become a weather forecaster. Piers then became a sceptic on global warming, denying that climate change is the product of human activity. He maintains it's to do with sunspots.

"We talk quite a lot. Don't always agree. It's a family, you know," said Jeremy.

Their brother, Andrew, is also "far to the left" of Jeremy. He became an expert in the oil business advising in Mozambique. When the country's Marxist President Samora Machel was killed in 1986, the cash-strapped Labour Party could not afford to send a representative and it fell to Andrew Corbyn to relate the party's condolences at the funeral.

Donald Anderson, MP for Swansea East and the party's foreign affairs spokesman responsible for Africa should have been there. Anderson had drawn up detailed plans to attend the funeral. The Foreign Office had offered assistance with accommodation in southern Africa and had arranged a programme of meetings with political figures. But when the MP went to the leader of the opposition's office in the Commons, party leader Neil Kinnock's staff said there was no spare cash to pay the £1,500 airfare.

Anderson then took his request to the Labour Party's headquarters at Walworth Road in south London and came away empty-handed. With nobody representing the party officially, it was left to Corbyn to pass a letter of condolence to the Mozambique foreign ministry.

"The whole business was quite humiliating," said a Labour source. "It was important for Anderson to go there because this kind of state event allows an invaluable opportunity for informal talks with senior politicians from many countries. Instead, we end up being represented by one of the Corbyn brothers."

Jeremy was educated at the prestigious Adams' Grammar School in Newport. Founded in 1656, during the protectorship of Oliver Cromwell, by William Adams, a wealthy member of the Worshipful Company of Haberdashers, a senior livery company in the City of London, it is one of the country's top boarding schools. Old boys include several senior politicians, but they are generally Conservatives. However, one Old Novaportan – as former pupils of Adams' Grammar dubbed themselves – who might have inspired the young Jeremy was Robert Charnook (1663–96). He was hanged after conspiring in an unsuccessful plot to kill William III near Turnham Green in February 1696. The blunderbuss he intended to use to assassinate the King is on display in the Tower of London.

One of the political figures Corbyn said he most admired also comes from that era.

"I think in English history a very interesting character is John Lilburne," he said. "Very interesting character, because of the way he managed to develop the whole debate about the English civil war into something very different. And there is a report that I can't find any proof of one way or the other, that in late 1648 he had a three-day parley with Cromwell at the Nag's Head in Islington. I can't find the record of it. But I wish I could get it. Then I could get a plaque put up for it."

Born in 1914, Lilburne was the leader of the Levellers, a radical democratic party that came to prominence. From the gentry, he joined the Puritans in their opposition to the Anglican High Church of Charles I. Caught smuggling Puritan pamphlets in from the Netherlands, he was tried before the Star Chamber, fined, publicly whipped, pilloried and jailed until freed by the Long Parliament, thanks to a motion introduced by Cromwell.

Becoming a captain in the Parliamentary army, he was captured and narrowly missed being tried for treason. Coining the term "free-born rights" – defining them as rights with which every human being is born, as opposed to rights bestowed by government or human law – he became known as "Free-born John". A tireless pamphleteer, he called for religious liberty, extension of the suffrage to craftsmen and small-property owners, and complete equality before the law. His works have been cited by the US Supreme Court.

The Levellers eventually fell foul of Cromwell's regime and Lilburne spent most of the period from 1645 to 1655 in jail, though he was twice acquitted of high treason. Released after converting to the Quaker faith, he died in 1657.

At Adams Grammar School in Newport, Jeremy was one of just two Labour supporters when the boys held a mock election in the run-up to the general election in 1964. His friend Bob Mallett recalled Corbyn being jeered by his right-wing schoolmates.

"Jeremy was the Labour candidate and I his campaign manager because at a middle-class boarding grammar school in leafy Shropshire, there weren't many socialists," said Mallett. "We were trounced."

Country-wide, the Labour Party won with just four seats after thirteen years of Tory rule and Harold Wilson became prime minister. But at school, Jeremy was swimming against the tide. A recent article by an Old Novaportan said that "racism, sexism and homophobia... are institutionalised within its walls".

Matthew Broomfield, writing in *The Oxford Tab*, said: "Adams' drilled into us that the strong were always superior to the weak. The ethos of self-advancement, self-protection and self-promotion was echoed everywhere from the assembly hall to the rugby field. The arrogant confidence I learnt at Adams' taught me to capitalise on my privilege. 'You are Adams' Boys' ran the endlessly repeated litany. We took it to mean 'you are better than those dirty little shits at the comprehensive – you are better than those below you in the exam tables or weaker than you on the rugby pitch- you are better than everyone else because you have beaten them – you are better because you are Adams' Boys.'"

Plainly this ethos did not rub off on Jeremy.

Unlike his brothers, Jeremy was a poor student, concerning himself instead with the burning issue of the time – ending the war in Vietnam. He denied been lazy at school. Rather he preferred to educate himself.

"I liked reading about things, doing my own course of study in that sense," he said.

He left school at eighteen with two A-levels, grade E, though he proudly admits that he was more qualified than John Major who only had O-levels.

University was not an option. Instead he worked on a local newspaper, then he did two years Voluntary Service Overseas in Jamaica which had just achieved its independence. It was, he said, "an amazing two years". He was a teacher in a deprived area of Kingston, while the north coast of the island remained the playground of the rich.

Fellow VSO worker Peter Croft was with Corbyn in Jamaica.

"They had gained their independence, but there were the vestiges of the colonial times," he said. "I remember that we had a talk from one of the embassy staff on the etiquette of responding to invitations to cocktail parties at the embassy. And I think even for us coming from England it was really a rather dramatic illustration of the contrast, in terms of privilege and relative deprivation. Going out to Jamaica at that time changed the way that we looked at the world and changed how we were when we came back to Britain."

Jeremy's time in Jamaica ingrained in him his rejection of all the values that public school had sought to instil; in the 1960s he struggled against what he saw, as imperialist attitudes, social division, economic exploitation became lifelong causes for Corbyn.

During his time in the Caribbean, he is insistent, he never did drugs. However, he did nurture some literary ambitions. He sent a poem to the *New Statesman* for publication.

"I never heard anything for months," said Corbyn, "and then it was eventually rejected."

Asked by the *News Stateman* when he was running for office whether he would still like them to publish it. He said enthusiastically: "Yes, I would."

Simon Fletcher, a former chief of staff for Ken Livingstone who sat in on the interview, intervened.

"We'd better see what's in it first," he said.

The poem has yet to appear in print.

Chapter Two – Apprenticeship in Politics

When Jeremy Corbyn returned from Jamaica, he studied briefly at the North London Polytechnic in the borough of Islington, where the prominent historian A.J.P. Taylor lectured. He dropped out without completing his degree when he rowed with his tutors about the syllabus.

"Jeremy had his studies terminated because he had big arguments with the people in charge," said his brother Piers. "He probably knew more than them."

Corbyn then became a full-time organizer in the National Union of Tailors and Garment Workers, but could do little to halt its long-term decline. Shedding members, the NUTGW merged into the GMB in 1991.

He continued his career in the trade union movement, working for the Amalgamated Engineering and Electrical Union, then the fifth biggest union in the country. He went on to become national organizer of NUPE – the National Union of Public Employees, now part of Unison which is one of his parliamentary sponsors.

Living in north London, he soon conformed to the leftist stereotype: ascetic and parsimonious, teetotal and vegetarian, insouciant about his dress and occasionally wearing a Lenin-style cap. He was also a member of the Campaign for Nuclear Disarmament, rising to become national vice-chair.

After serving on the public health authority, in 1974, at the age of just twenty-five, Corbyn was elected to Haringey Council and became secretary of the North Islington Labour Party. Looking back on his relations with members of the constituency party forty years later, he said: "North Islington is a wonderful place, it's incredibly tolerant, particularly of me and I'm very grateful to everyone in Islington for support over the years and particularly to people in North Islington Labour party who have probably disagreed with me at some point on something, perhaps everyone at some point disagrees with me on something, and some people disagree with me on everything all of the time but we're still there together so it kind of works."

That same year he married twenty-four-year-old Jane Chapman, then a fellow Labour Party activitist in Haringey, who described Corbyn as her "political soul-mate". Their whirlwind romance took place during Labour's 1974 election campaign. There were no candle-lit dinners, but plenty of political meetings.

"It was a youthful romance," said Jane. "We were soul-mates in the party, both in our twenties. I stood for parliament twice in the 1970s and Jeremy was the agent for Hornsey. He worked for NUPE, the public service trade union. I was working on my PhD. And then there was politics in the evening. Every evening there would be meetings."

They married in Haringey Town Hall, but there was also a celebration at Jane's Tory-supporting father's bowling club in Weston-super-Mare. Afterwards it was straight back to work campaigning.

Party colleagues likened them to a junior version of Aneurin "Nye" Bevan and Jennie Lee – the married socialist MPs beloved as heroes of the Labour left in the post-war years, though it now appears that their marriage was riven with infidelity.

"We both got elected to Haringey Council in 1974," said Jane. "Politics became our life. He was out most evenings because when we weren't at meetings he would go to the Labour headquarters, and do photocopying – in those days you couldn't print because there were no computers."

Corbyn was already a strict vegetarian.

"He would eat anything as long as it wasn't meat," she said. "He had quite a good appetite, but he didn't mind what the food was because he couldn't be bothered to give it the time. So he would just grab a can of beans and eat it straight from the can."

According to Jane, attending a political meeting was his idea of a good night out.

"Yes, that was relaxation," she said. "Talking politics is relaxation."

There was precious little time off. Just occasionally he would indulge his love of travel.

"It would be unfair to say that he had no interests outside politics," Jane said. "We did go on holiday in August, when politics closes down. We went on his 250cc motorbike, with me on the back, and we rode right across Europe several times."

It was a Czech CZ bike and they camped out in a little two-person tent.

"We travelled through France into Switzerland, Germany, Austria, and from there into Czechoslovakia and to what is now Slovakia."

Otherwise life was comfortable.

"We had a garden where we lived," said Jane. "We had chickens. We were a bit like *The Good Life*. We had a cat and a dog. The cat was called Harold, after Harold Wilson, and mongrel was called Mango."

But even Sunday evenings would be taken up with meetings at Tony Benn's house. Jane sometimes went along too.

"I can remember going to Tony Benn's house with Jeremy for a party and being ever so impressed because the toilet was full of books," she said. "I had never been in a toilet before that was full of books. He was very much a father figure to the left-wing."

Politically Tony Benn was a father figure to Corbyn, who stuck with Benn until his death in 2014 and remains the torch carrier for the Bennite cause. Both were teetotal and vegetarians.

Jeremy and Jane split in 1979, the year Mrs Thatcher became prime minister, when she eventually tired of the relentless nature of his political activism.

"I got burnt out by politics, I was exhausted by it all and he wasn't," she said. "I decided towards the end that I really wanted to do some of the normal things for twenty-something-year-olds, like going to the cinema and going out dancing and that kind of thing, you know."

She could not persuade him to do that. He had few interests outside politics then, but more recently he has taken to woodturning, making bowls and chopping boards which he gives as gifts.

"I missed the other things," she said. "We didn't do things that I liked such as going to the cinema or to clubs. I wanted a different work-life balance."

She had married Corbyn for his "honesty" and "principles", but his intense dedication to Left-wing politics eventually became too much.

"He has remained very focused politically but, although I was committed, I just didn't have it to the same extent," said Jane.

She complained that as he devoted "100 percent" to politics, there was not much left for her. She was also unhappy that he, at that stage, told her he did not want children. Even their break-up was political.

"When I left him, one of his final words was to tell me to 'read Simone de Beauvoir,' she said.

Piers said their marriage ended because Jane, who became a university lecture, and "non-academic" Jeremy were not suited. Nevertheless she remained on good terms with her ex-husband.

"He's very principled, very honest, he doesn't drink, he doesn't smoke and you'd never find any financial impropriety," she said when she heard he was running for the leadership of the Labour Party. "He is a genuinely nice guy."

She went on to become a professor at Lincoln University, specializing in communications. Still a member of the Labour Party, she voted for him the the Labour leadership contest and remains a fan.

"He's really shaken politics in this country. He's pulling in bigger crowds than Tony Blair."

Corbyn worked on Tony Benn's unsuccessful campaign to become deputy leader of the Labour Party in 1981. The time seemed opportune as Michael Foot had been elected leader the previous year and the party had moved to the left – so much so that some of the social democratic wing of the party quit to form the SDP, which later formed an alliance with the Liberals. Benn had strong support among the membership but, at that time, they only had thirty percent of the votes in the deputy leadership contest. The Parliamentary Labour Party had another thirty percent, while affiliated trades unions had forty percent. The PLP and the unions both backed the incumbent Denis Healey, who beat Benn by 50.4 percent to 49.6.

But Corbyn was already an unshakeable Bennite.

"He was an original thinker," said Corbyn, "and also I think very bravely published his diaries, which showed his developing original thought. And yeah, he got the most amazing attacks and was ridiculed throughout his life but ended up a much-loved, old-school institution. Tony was a legend, in many, many ways."

Like Benn, Corbyn supported the abolition of the UK's independent nuclear deterrent, saying "nuclear weapons are immoral". He also favoured withdrawal from Nato, saying "I'd rather we weren't in it". These were issues that contributed to the Labour split in 1981. At the time he was a hard-line eurosceptic, he favoured pulling out, though he later softened his line on Brexit, saying that Britain should not walk away, but rather "fight together for a better Europe".

In 1981, when Ken Livingstone was planning his coup to take over the leadership of the Greater London Council he named Jeremy Corbyn, then a NUPE regional officer, as one of his key allies on the executive. They too became close political allies when both were in parliament.

Corbyn was also a key player in the NUPE's dispute with the NHS over planned government cuts in 1982. He was then organizer for London and took Tony Benn to St Mary's Hospital in Paddington where there were around 150 people at a meeting to prepare the ground for a day of action.

"They are determined not to have the NHS destroyed," said Benn.

Chapter Three – The Campaign Group

In 1982, Jeremy Corbyn was selected as Labour Party candidate for Islington North. The following June, Margaret Thatcher won the most decisive election victory since the Labour landslide of 1945. From being one of the most unpopular prime ministers in history, she had won the election on the back of Britain's victory in the Falklands War. While the country shunned Michael Foot and swung violently to the right, Corbyn won with a majority of 9,657, taking 50 percent of the vote. Islington North had been a solid Labour constituency since 1937, but in the face of a national collapse, Corbyn managed to increase the Labour vote by 9.6 percent.

In parliament Corbyn joined the Socialist Campaign Group, immediately identifying him as one of the more left-wing MPs. The Campaign Group had been formed the previous December by supporters of Tony Benn who quit the leftist Tribune group after Benn's failure to win the deputy leadership. Corbyn has remained a member ever since, alongside the likes of Dennis Skinner, Tony Banks and Diane Abbott. Corbyn further proved his left-wing credentials by becoming a weekly columnist for the *Morning Star*, the left-wing newspaper that called itself "The People's Daily".

After the election, Tony Benn was at a meeting at Chris Mullin's flat in Brixton to discuss what had gone wrong.

"Most of our friends were there – Tom Sawyer, Jeremy Corbyn, Audrey Wise, Ann Pettifor, Francis Prideaux, Les Huckfield, Michael Meacher, Tony Banks, Mandy Moore, Frances Morrell, Reg Race, Jon Lansman, Jo Richardson, Stuart Holland, Alan Meale, Ken Livington," said Benn.

They sat in the garden of Mullin's flat holding their post mortem.

"Jeremy Corbyn (who is now MP for Islington North) didn't want a binge of recrimination," wrote Benn in his diaries. "The campaign had started well and then everything had been fudged. We had the support of traditional Labour in the inner cities, the ethnic vote, middle-class activists and pensioners."

As ever, Corbyn did not pull his punches.

"There was great incompetence in the Party machine," he said. "The leaflets put out were absolutely bland crap."

Neil Kinnock, though a left-winger himself and Foot's Shadow Secretary of State for Education and Science, was singled out for blame.

"Kinnock lost the deputy leadership for Tony in 1981 deliberately and specifically, and he was busy preparing himself for the leadership campaign during the General Election," Corbyn told the Campaign Group. "There must be a left candidate. Heffer is a candidate, he is against the witch-hunt, and I think we should consider him."

When Michael Foot stood down as party leader, Tony Benn could not stand because he had lost his seat in the election. Eric Heffer, a former member of the Communist Party of Great Britain and one-time admirer of Stalin, stood as the candidate of the "hard left". He received minimal support among the trade unions and constituency parties, and came third among Labour MPs, obtaining 6.3 percent of the electoral college. Neil Kinnock won the party leadership with 71 percent of the vote.

No fan of Kinnock, Corbyn was critical of the soft stance the Labour Party was taking, particularly as pit closures were going ahead and the miners' strike was looming.

"There is some equivocation in the Party," said Corbyn. "People are saying that the job of the PLP is to go for the middle-class suburban vote, but the Campaign Group must be on the picket lines and at the workplace level. In inner-city areas where there are no major employers except local government and some public services, there just isn't trade union experience, and school-leavers know nothing about the trade union or labour movement."

Some were shocked at how radical he could be. Former Islington Labour councillor Leo McKintrisy, who spent ten years in the local party, recalled: "Even in the 1980s, we would have described him as on the far left. One time we were talking about economic policy and he was criticizing Neil Kinnock for being too soft. He said, very triumphantly, 'Our job is not to reform capitalism, it's to overthrow it.' And I thought that was a bizarre statement for someone who was a MP for a mainstream centre-left party."

In 1984, he was arrested for protesting against apartheid outside South Africa House, along with Tony Banks and Stuart Holland.

Corbyn was carrying a placard that said: "Defend the right to demonstrate against apartheid – join this picket."

Explaining what had happened in the House of Commons, he said: "It was one of these strange moments when you are arrested by the police and you say: 'Under what charge am I being arrest.' Assuming one is going to be told 'obstruction'. They said no. It was under the Diplomatic Immunities Act. It was behaviour that was offensive to a foreign diplomatic mission. And the police officer said to me what do you plead and why have you come here? I said: 'I have come here to be as offensive as possible to the South African apartheid regime, but I offer no plea so you will have to offer a plea on my part of Not Guilty.' The cases all went to court and we were all exonerated on the grounds of our moral outrage at apartheid, all given compensation and all that compensation was given to the ANC and the Anti-Apartheid Movement."

Corbyn also served on the executive of the Anti-Apartheid Movement and he joined Tony Benn as a patron of the Palestine Solidarity Campaign.

He courted controversy again by joining Ken Livingstone, then leader of the Greater London Council, inviting Sinn Féin President Gerry Adams to speak in London in 1984, weeks after the IRA had blown up the Grand Hotel in Brighton during the Conservative Party Conference, nearly killing Prime Minister Margaret Thatcher.

Corbyn always took a special interest in Ireland. In April 1985, he and Tony Benn flew to Belfast to sit in the so-called "supergrass" trials. These were trials held without juries where the verdict was given by a single judge sitting alone in a "Diplock" court. Informers from both nationalist and loyalist organizations would then give uncorroborated evidence against individuals allegedly involved in paramilitary activity in returned for police protection, immunity from prosecution and, sometimes, cash. Many convictions resulting from supergrasss evidence were found to be unsafe and were subsequently overturned.

While Corbyn and Benn were queuing for the public gallery a court official recognized two MPs and, explaining that the public gallery's screen was badly scratched and the speakers broken, offered to seat them inside the court. When they were ushered into the well of the court, there were no seats available. But as the trial was being heard by a judge alone, the court officer offered them a perch in the jury box.

The republican defendant must have thought all his dreams had come true. Spotting the pair, the defence barrister announced to the judge: "I'm surprised how small the new jury is but I'm happy to accept their verdict instead of yours."

Corbyn remained an active supporter of the union movement. In August 1985, he spoke at a march to Islington Town Hall to support 450 members of Nalgo – the National and Local Government Officers' Association – who had been on strike since August 5, to force the council to honour its commitment against racism. The dispute, said to be the first of its type involving local government workers on such a scale, arose after black members of staff were allegedly denied participation in social events and access to essential information for their work and subjected to racist remarks. The remaining members of Nalgo were due to strike in protest against alleged racial harassment within the housing department.

With Tony Benn and the rest of the Campaign Group, he voted against the 1985 Anglo-Irish Agreement, which sought to bring an end to the Troubles in Ulster, but give the Eire government an advisory role in the government of Northern Ireland. It also confirmed that there would be no change in the constitutional position of Northern Ireland unless a majority of its people agreed to join the Republic, though it set out conditions for the establishment of a devolved consensus government in the region. Approved by a margin of 473 to 47 against, it got the biggest majority during Thatcher's premiership.

The Labour Party was in turmoil; the growing influence of the Militant Tendency, a Trotskyist which had taken over Liverpool City Council, was threatening the seats of moderate candidates. One of those they had in their sights was Robert Kilroy-Silk, the Labour MP for Knowsley North on Merseyside who later became a chat-show host and a UKIP MEP. Corbyn was sanguine about any attack from the left. The result was a famous confrontation in the House of Commons.

"I had been on a programme on television the day before talking about why Militants shouldn't be expelled from the Labour party," said Corbyn. "He thought they should, and he was extremely abusive, threw me against a wall in the voting lobby. His quote was: 'I'm an amateur boxer, I can sort anybody out,' and somebody said to me what do you do in your spare time, and I said: 'I'm an amateur runner,' which is true. I do enjoy running."

But he denied running away.

"I walked off," he said. "You can hardly run through the voting lobby. He thought it was a great triumph for his macho prowess."

Kilroy-Silk told another story in *The Times*. He had been upset about Corbyn's appearance in Michael Cockerel's TV film where he had made remarks about a "healthy debate" that was going on in Kilroy-Silk's constituency. This was after Kilroy-Silk had claimed to have been assaulted by members of the Militant there.

He called Corbyn a "rat".

"Jeremy Corbyn was the one who made me ablaze," said Kilroy-Silk. "Oh, he declared, nothing to worry about here. All got up by the media. It's the media, the ex-public schoolboy said, that's created all this, they've created the 'conflict', the 'division', the 'strife'. The bastard, he even cast doubts both on Cockerell's integrity and, more important, on the Knowsley women's credibility by suggesting that the reporter had 'looked long' to get that kind of quote. He hadn't looked at all. The comments were thrust at him by decent Labour women."

Kilroy-Silk said after seeing the programme he searched the Commons looking for Corbyn, eventually catching up with him during a vote on the Transport Bill.

"Two days later, I saw Corbyn in the division lobby," said Kilroy-Silk. "I'd been looking for him in the Commons all day. I was talking to Barry Sheerman and John Evans, the MP for St Helen's

North, strategically placed near the exit through which all Labour MPs would have to pass."

When Evans noticed that Kilroy-Silk was distracted he complained: "You're not listening."

"I'm looking for Corbyn," Kilroy-Silk said. "I want a word with him."

"Oh Christ," said Evan.

"You know what it's about?"

"Oh aye," said Evans. "Look Rob, whatever you do, don't hit him."

Kilroy-Silk recalled that was the last thing his wife had said to him when he left home that morning.

"I was about to tell him that when I saw Corbyn walking towards us with Michael Meacher from the far end of the wide green-carpeted, book-lined corridor," said Kilroy-Silk. "I strode towards them."

"Remember," Evans called from behind, "don't hit him."

"Hello, mate," said Corbyn as Kilroy-Silk bore down on him.

"Don't you 'mate' me," snapped Kilroy-Silk.

Meacher disappeared, but Kilroy-Silk said he blocked Corbyn's escape.

"Since when have you been an expert on my constituency, eh?" he asked. "Since when have you been qualified to pontificate on television about it? So it was all just 'healthy debate', was it? Well, how do you like some healthy debate?"

Kilroy-Silk boasted later: "I didn't really hit him. If I had, he'd have stayed down."

There was, however, "a robust exchange of views".

"I don't remember how long I 'spoke' to him," said Kilroy-Silk. "I do remember that I said all that I wanted to say and that he became aware of my displeasure. The creep. There must have been upwards of two hundred Labour MPs in the lobby at the time, but no one attempted to intervene and no one said a word. I learnt afterwards that that was because most of them were waiting, hoping for me to hit him. There was, apparently, a great demand for the video of the film afterwards and several showings were provided in the Whips' Office."

Failing to stay for the vote, Kilroy-Silk got home in time to watch *News at Ten*.

"At the end, Alistair Burnet said that there had been a scuffle between two Labour MPs in the lobby and quoted Corbyn as saying that I was a boxer and he was a runner, so he ran," said Kilroy-Silk. "I couldn't believe it. How could he say that about himself?"

Afterwards the phone started ringing.

"I was surprised," said Kilroy-Silk. "I hadn't really expected it to get out, certainly not so soon, and certainly not to evoke the interest that it seems to have attracted. This time I corroborated the story. If Corbyn is going to go around telling everyone about it, as he seems to have done, then I am determined to get my view across."

After Kilroy-Silk sent a letter off to *The Times* about it, he noticed that there was a lot of press coverage on the incident under such headlines as the *Daily Mirror*'s "Punch-up MP does it again" and the Guardian's more subtle "Division of Labour".

"The press accounts, obviously emanating from Corbyn, not only describe the air as 'very thick with four-letter words', but also claim that I was seen to 'draw back my fist' and had to be restrained," complained Kilroy-Silk. "It's not true. I didn't draw back my fist and no-one would have wanted to restrain me. The story that Sean Hughes, my neighbour in Knowsley South, told me about the Chief Whip, Michael Cocks, was typical. 'I thought Bob was really going to hit him,' Sean said to Mike. 'There's plenty of time yet,' Mike answered hopefully."

Kilroy-Silk was not the only one to criticize Corbyn for not taking the opportunity to speak out against Militant. In a *Guardian* article by Tom Gallagher, Labour MP for Bradford South, condemned him for failing "to utter one word of support for a colleague fighting off a bid by the Militant Tendency to oust him". He added that Corbyn's appearance on Cockerel's programme "did a bad day's work for the Labour cause".

Militant's influence waned after they were attacked by Neil Kinnock at the 1985 Labour Party Conference. Eric Heffer MP, a member of the Socialist Campaign Group, walked off the platform during Kinnock's speech. Fellow member Dennis Skinner, then on the Labour Party's National Executive Committee, also opposed an investigation into Militant's activities. Two members of the Campaign Group – Dave Nellist and Terry Fields – were expelled from the Labour Party for being members of Militant.

Chapter Four – A Thorn in the Side

Corbyn may have been a thorn in the side of his parliamentary colleagues, but he was a stickler for the protocols of the House. In February 1986 he demanded in the Commons that Geoffrey Dickens, Conservative MP for Littleborough and Saddleworth should go to the Holbrooke Estate in North Islington, unreservedly withdraw his allegations of the existence of child brothels in the area and make a public apology. Corbyn noted that there had been a breach of the Commons convention that members should not visit another constituency without notifying the local MP.

One of the conventions of the House he embraced was vituperative attacks on the government. Discussing the plight of the elderly over heating costs, Norman Fowler, Secretary of State for Social Services, said that the government should stop regarding pensioners as a problem and look at them as people who had made an enormous contribution to society and did not wish to be patronized.

David Waddington, Minister of State at the Home Office was asked: "What is an individual immigrant family supposed to do if their own MP either has views that are so racist they cannot approach him or refuses to take up any immigration cases?"

In 1986, during prime minister's questions, Corbyn described Margaret Thatcher's Secretary of State of Education and Science –

and her political mentor – Sir Keith Joseph as a "lame duck". He stepped down soon after.

That June, Corbyn was among sixteen people arrested outside the Old Bailey in a protest against the strip search of women defendants in a bomb trial. When he returned to the house, Timothy Eggar, Under Secretary of State for Foreign and Commonwealth Affairs, said that he was pleased to see Corbyn taking part in the democratic process rather than demonstrating on the streets.

Corbyn later asked if Eggar thought that MPs who took part in demonstrations outside the House were acting undemocratically.

"Does not democracy mean that people have a right to speak freely in this House and also a right to speak freely and demonstrate outside the House on matters they feel strongly about?" he said.

The Speaker, Bernard Weatherill, said: "I am not responsible for what Mr Corbyn does outside the House but it is perfectly in order for him to demonstrate if that is what he wishes to do. But every MP takes responsibility for what he says here."

Conservative MP Antony Marlow then asked the Speaker if he would confirm that, although any MP was entitled to demonstrate or speak freely, he was not entitled to break the law.

"I have not been charged with any offence arising from any actions which took place outside the Old Bailey," Corbyn pointed out.

He drew more protests when he said the Government should improve DHSS advice services instead of attacking local authorities and claimants' organizations to pay for tax cuts and the Royal

Wedding of Prince Andrew and Sarah Ferguson. With hindsight, many would have agreed.

Corbyn was also prepared to take on the press. Defending local authorities against the secretary of state who attacked local authorities that attempted to do anything to meet the needs of their community or to redress the imbalance inherent in society, he said in December 1986: "Over the past four years, there had been a systematic process of media attacks on individual local authorities. Haringey had been crawled over by journalists from the Murdoch empire, day after day scratching for dirt and salacious gossip, camping around the gardens of houses where Labour councillors lived and following them. There had been a series of untrue newspaper stories concerning actions that councils had supposedly taken."

The government had supported the smear campaign, he maintained.

"This marauding band of gutter journalists wander round the country just looking for lies to print about Labour councils," he said. Meanwhile they were hushing up what the Tory and Liberal councils were up to.

Striking a back, Corbyn said that school children in Berkshire who paid for their schooling were getting a proper Christmas lunch while those on free school meals got bangers and mash. That was the kind of policy pursued by Conservative-controlled councils, he said. Lambeth had a better record than Wandsworth, he maintained, with lower rate and rent rises and more new homes being built. Yet it was

31

the Lambeth councillors who had been surcharged and thrown out of office.

Corbyn had the Murdoch press in his sights particularly at the time as he was spending his nights picketing the new News International plant in Wapping, after *The Times*, *The Sunday Times*, *The Sun* and the *News of the World* moved there to escape the "Spanish practices" of Fleet Street. Dismissal notices were served on all those taking part in the ensuing industrial action, effectively sacking thousands of employees.

"The News International dispute was an example of an oppressive government which paid thousands of police officers to keep five thousand people out of work," Corbyn told the House. "Because of inadequate industrial relations legislation, a private employer had been allowed to dismiss people at will and the Government supported him."

He joined Tony Benn and Diane Abbott, then prospect Labour candidate for Hackney North and Stoke Newington, on the platform, making speeches outside the works. It was a bitter dispute and dragged on for over a year. Corbyn said he had seen police line up in ranks there, as if preparing for a medieval battle. Over a thousand arrests were made and nine people died. The strike eventually collapsed in February 1987.

During the strike Corbyn had also been busy elsewhere. On 15 April 1986, the United States Air Force had bombed Libya, ostensibly in retaliation for the bombing of a Berlin nightclub where an American serviceman was killed. The US bombers had taken off from airbases in the UK. Muammar Gaddafi's adopted daughter was among the casualties. In response, Corbyn, Benn and pacifist peer Fenner Brockway formed the Campaign for Non-Alignment in Britain. Corbyn and Benn provided a forward to Ben Lowe's *Peace Through Non-Alignment: The Case Against British Membership of NATO*, published the following year.

Although there had been concerns in the House about the abuse of early day motions, Corbyn was happy to table them when he felt strongly about a matter. Just to show that he was not entirely humourless, he put down an early day motion on 9 December 1986 which said: "That this House congratulates the canteen workers of the Refreshment Department on the production of an excellent bean casserole on December 4/5, welcomes the availability of vegetarian food; and hopes that in future there will be a wide variety of wholefood and vegetarian dishes."

However, Corbyn did take these matters seriously. Under the ten-minute-rule procedure, he introduced the Abolition of Deer Hunting bill in June 1990 which aimed to ban the hunting and killing of deer with dogs. He said that the bill would strengthen animal protection legislation by prohibiting "a vile and barbaric bloodsport which was born out of bloodlust". As for animal experimentation, he said: "This is a secretive, barbaric practice which should have no place in a civilised society." The following year introduced a bill against hare coursing.

Corbyn was often under attack because of his belief in a united Ireland. In January 1987, twenty-nine-year-old Sean O'Regan pleaded guilty to fraud, making bomb-hoax statements and attempted robbery in the Old Bailey. He claimed to have approached Corbyn in the House of Commons, posing as an IRA bomber who wanted to flee the country. It was reported that Corbyn gave him £45. The Central Criminal Court was told that O'Regan was a "clever confidence trickster". He was jailed for four years. In fact it was a member of staff at Corbyn's constituency office who had given O'Regan the money. When Corbyn found out about the incident he immediately notified the police.

However, he did employ Ronan Bennett, an IRA supporter, as a research assistant. In 1975, Bennett had received a life sentence for the murder of an RUC police inspector. After serving thirteen months in prison in Belfast, his conviction was quashed by appeal court judges who ruled that the identification evidence which helped convict him was unreliable. Following his release he came to England and in 1977 was arrested in a Special Branch raid in Huddersfield. A week later he successfully appealed against an exclusion order under the Prevention of Terrorism Act which would have deported him to Ulster. In 1979, along with three other members of the Black Flag anarchist group, Bennett was acquitted of conspiracy charges in a controversial trial at the Old Bailey.

When the House of Commons' Serjeant-at-Arms stripped Bennett of his House of Commons' pass, Corbyn protested, saying that Bennett had been proved innocent by two courts and that the removal of his Commons pass would be "a disgraceful attack and character assassination of an innocent man".

"The speaker appears to be bowing to pressure from the government," said Corbyn. "There also seems to be an implicit degree of pressure coming from the security services who want to vet all parliamentary staff. If they are allowed to carry this through, the vetting of all parliamentary candidates will be the next move... I will be seeking an immediate meeting with the speaker tomorrow and insisting that he reinstate Ronan Bennett 's pass. I have also contacted Labour's chief whip and have every confidence that I will be receiving the full backing of parliamentary colleagues. We will fight this all the way."

Corbyn went on to insist that Bennett was "a well-respected academic, a research fellow of the Institute of Historical Research and has recently completed a PhD thesis. He is a thoroughly capable individual".

"His research work for me centres on the Prevention of Terrorism Act," said Corbyn. "Any attempt to remove Ronan's pass would be an attack on the rights of all MPs' assistants."

Security fears that Bennett was a link between the Provisional IRA and left-wing Labour MPs were "utterly ridiculous", Corbyn insisted.

Bennett went on to complete his PhD and became a respected novelist.

While being recognized as one of the most hard-working members of parliament, Corbyn had the temerity to appear in the House for the second reading of the Finance Bill without wearing a jacket or a tie – a state of undress that drew a shower of criticism from Conservative MPs.

"What I do and say is more important than what I look like," he said in his defence.

In February 1987, he accused the Department of Energy of deliberately under-funding research into alternative sources of energy to lead to the conclusion that only nuclear power could solve the problems. That August he further embarrassed the government over the book *Spycatcher*, the banned memoirs of MI6 operative Peter Wright, pointing out that it was hypocritical to ban the book when copies were freely available in the House of Commons library.

"The best way of exposing the hypocrisy of this government is to publish extracts in all the papers," he told a meeting of three hundred people organized by the Campaign for Press and Broadcasting Freedom in the Conway Hall.

Comedians Terry Jones, Michael Palin and Rik Mayall, and various trade unionists, read from the book, while Paul McCartney sent a tape recorded reading to the meeting.

In October 1987, there were calls for Labour Party members to boycott the Chesterfield Socialist Conference.

"I did think that was funny," said Tony Benn, then MP for Chesterfield.

He, Paul Foot, Ken Livingstone, Arthur Scargill and other stalwarts turned out. Jeremy Corbyn gave a workshop on foreign affairs. He sat alongside Benn when he proposed forging a genuine left-wing alternative to Thatcherism.

Corbyn said he hoped the Chesterfield conference would succeed in turning the Labour Party into a force demanding socialism "rather than the retreatism that people see at the present time". Criticizing Kinnock's "yuppification" of the Labour Party, he accused the leader's "everything up for grabs" policy review.

"Our aim is to put socialism back on the agenda," said Corbyn. "There is a lack of clarity to the party's strategy."

Corbyn was one of the thirteen MPs behind the magazine *Labour Briefing* which attacked Kinnock's "kamikaze" style of leadership. He also attacked Kinnock's anti-Soviet stance.

"The party's defence document was so festooned with the Union Jack as to be easily confused with a Ministry of Defence hand-out," he said. Meanwhile, the policy review was "born out of despair and a belief that reading the entrails of opinion polls is all that is required".

He was equally as scathing of the Conservatives. When they introduced a bill extending the right to vote to UK citizens living abroad, he said that it showed how concerned the Tory Party had become about its future, if it had to go around the world looking for tax dodgers, crooks, thieves and wasters. And he created more outrage among parliamentarians when he observed a minute's silence for the eight IRA members killed by the SAS in an ambush.

But there were more intimate matters on Corbyn's agenda. In 1987, he married left-wing Chilean campaigner Claudia Bracchitta. She was an exile when they met through his work with Amnesty International and the campaign against the Chilean dictator Augusto Pinochet. He told the House of Commons that people were being gunned down in the streets in Chile and the British government was on the side of the murderers. They set up home in Finsbury Park.

Despite her concerns about her homeland, Claudia was not a political wife. Few colleagues in the House of Commons even realized he was married. She was very much of the left. Later Corbyn was asked whether he could imagine having a relationship with somebody who wasn't on the left.

"No. At the end of the day, it's the question of your values," he said. "They get in the way."

Corbyn was a campaigner for the Guildford Four and the Birmingham Six until their convictions for the 1974 pub bombings were quashed by the Court of Appeal in 1989 and 1991 respectively. He regularly visited Paul Hill who was sentenced to nine life sentences for the Guildford and Woolwich pub bombings.

Tabling a Commons motion congratulating Hill on his marriage to Marion Serravalli in the Roman Catholic chapel of Long Lartin prison in 1988, he said: "I have been visiting Paul for four years because he comes from my constituency and I'm convinced he's innocent." He travelled to the prison to attend the wedding.

When Hill was finally released on bail in October 1989 pending a fresh inquiry, Corbyn provided a surety of £2,000. Hill went on to write his autobiography with the help of Ronan Bennett who, by then, had admitted to being a full-time member of the Anarchist movement in Britain. Divorcing Serravalli, Hill married Courtney Kennedy, daughter of the assassinated Bobby, in 1992.

In 1989, Corbyn complained to a meeting of the Campaign Group that the Labour Party was not serious about opposing the poll tax. He turned out with Tony Benn and George Galloway at a rally in Trafalgar Square in March 1990. Benn estimated that there were 150,000 people there and the square was absolutely crammed. But before Corbyn could speak, the rally was stopped because of trouble. Following scuffles, mounted police in riot gear moved it. During prolonged rioting, buildings and cars were set alight. Around 113 were injured and 339 people were arrested.

Corbyn was one of the thirty Labour MPs who refused to pay the poll tax, went to court over it and was nearly jailed. Columnists have later compared him to Wat Tyler.

In 1990 Corbyn collaborated with Tony Benn in a secret tribute to suffragette Emily Wilding Davison. In Benn's diaries, he notes: "Tuesday 8 May: Jeremy Corbyn and I had a bite to eat, and then went down to the Commons Crypt with a Black & Decker drill and brass plaque commemorating Emily Wilding Davison. We screwed it on the door, in place of the temporary notice I had put up with Miss Frampton's help."

Davison had hidden in the broom cupboard there on the night of the census in 1911, so that she could give her place of residence that night as the "House of Commons". Two years later, she ran onto the racetrack at Epsom Downs and was trampled to death by the king's horse. Miss Frampton worked in the Serjeant-at-Arms office and had shown them the way to the broom cupboard down the secret stairs they did not even know existed.

While the party continued its policy review, readying itself for a general election, Corbyn was in despair that they were losing their core support in the country.

"People are not coming into the party, fewer people are coming to meetings, and there is a very low level of public activity in general," he said. "The party has not got a healthy base. It is all very shallow."

As for Labour's "new agenda", Corbyn was scathing.

"It's soft-soap populism. We do our opinion polls, find out what people want, and say 'OK, you can have it', without asking what kind of society we have now, and what kind of society we want to replace it."

Meanwhile there were hard political questions to tackle after Iraq invaded Kuwait in August 1990. When it became clear that a US-led coalition was going to drive Saddam Hussein out of Kuwait, Corbyn went to Quaker Peace Centre for a meeting with Tony Benn, Diane Abbott, Bernie Grant, Bruce Kent, Majorie Thompson of CND and others to discuss the Gulf crisis. They opposed this and had a long talk about whether they should have detailed objectives in trying to stop the war build-up. There was also concern that the United Nations was being used to legalize an American attack on Iraq. Although there was some tension in the meeting, they agreed to hold a press conference that Friday to launch their "Stop the War in the Gulf" campaign. Corbyn then took the time to speak out passionately against the arms trade at a meeting of the Campaign Group at the Wessex Hotel.

At a meeting of the Campaign Group in the House of Commons, Benn circulated a motion which he thought had the broad agreement of the Stop the War campaign. It said that they condemned the aggression, supported the sanctions and said that there was a prospect of a peaceful settlement. Further they would not authorize British military action without a special resolution by the UN and they would decline to support the government in the absence of such a declaration.

Benn said he was not surprised that there was a lot of argument about his resolution and was particularly concerned about Corbyn's reaction.

"Jeremy Corbyn was doubtful because of the UN, and thought we should say simply, 'Get out of the Gulf'," said Benn. "I should have cleared it with Jeremy first, because we are both officers of the Campaign Group."

Corbyn was secretary. In the end, most of them signed Benn's resolution.

Chapter Five – Friends on the Left

That December 1990 Jeremy Corbyn and his new wife Claudia attended a dinner at the Commons with Tony and Caroline Benn, celebrating his fortieth year in parliament. They sang "Happy Birthday". The Corbyns and the Benns were close and the family would visit the Benn country seat, "an ungainly, rambling 1920s house in a stunning location" near the hamlet of Stansgate in Essex.

In 1991, Tony Benn records: "Saturday 10 August, Stansgate: Up early, working in the garage on my Black & Decker work bench. At twelve o'clock Jeremy Corbyn and Claudia and little Ben and Sebastian arrived. It was again another perfect day at Stansgate, which makes a hell of a difference, and we had lunch. We went around a nature reserve and Jeremy enjoyed that very much. Took some photographs and then after tea everybody returned to London."

Jeremy was also a regular visitor to Benn's ramshackle Regency mansion in Holland Park, west London. He was there on 15 September 1991 for a Sunday evening meeting of the Independent Left Corresponding Society, a left-wing think tank which usually met every Sunday evening and, Benn said, "tried to carry the socialist message over the very dark years of Thatcherism". It was the first in sometime because Ralph Miliband – the Marxist father of David and Ed – had been ill and Benn had not wanted to have a meeting without him. That morning's paper had shown that Labour was lagging behind the Tories in the polls and Neil Kinnock was wildly unpopular. The talk in the meeting was that "Kinnock was an embarrassment, he was inconsistent, he was also a gabbler."

That December, Corbyn spoke out against the visit of Jean Marie le Pen, leader of France's National Front.

"Le Pen promotes race hatred and his purpose here is to set up a network of fascists," he said. Corbyn also remarked that it was ironic that Home Secretary Kenneth Baker had failed to halt the deportation of an asylum seeker from Zaire, but was allowing Monsieur Le Pen to visit Britain.

Joining the protest outside the Sheraton Park Hotel where Le Pen was staying, Corbyn said: "We are here to oppose Jean Marie Le Pen's visit. It's part of an attempt by him to set up a pan-European ultra-right network... He is a fascist, and if given any space to organize will try to organize a European fascist movement."

Corbyn sat on the Social Security Select Committee from 1992 to 1997. Opposing the Child Support Agency, set up to collect money from absentee fathers, he said: "The agency is entirely misguided. It has admitted that only £50 million of the £530 million it expects to raise from fathers in its first year will actually go to their children. The rest goes to the Treasury. Those who are not paying the CSA's demands are doing it in protest at this ludicrous system. Those who do pay are being pauperized."

When the Americans, British and French bombed Iraq in January 1993, Corbyn rushed to the House of Commons to condemn the action. He stood alongside Tony Benn, Bernie Grant, Tam Dalyell,

George Galloway and Bob Cryer, who was dubbed "a friend and ally of Saddam". But Corbyn was no George Galloway – he had been among the first to warn of the dangers of arming the Iraqi dictator.

Then in March, Corbyn had a meeting about a "World Appeal" to leaders, on peace and war, development, human rights and poverty. Benn found himself in charge of writing letters.

At the Sinn Féin press conference in the House of Commons in January 1994, the National Chairperson of Sinn Féin, Tom Hartley, turned up with Joan O'Connell, Gerry McLoughlin and Gerry Fitzpatrick to outline their reaction to the peace process going on between British Prime Minister John Major and Irish Taoiseach Albert Reyolds.

"Jeremy Corbyn and I talked with them in the cafeteria downstairs," said Benn. "Then we went into the Jubilee Room, had got there about half an hour early and it was packed with television people.... Lady Olga Maitland MP turned up and said: 'When will the violence stop?'"

Ever willing to back unpopular causes, in February 1994, Corbyn turned out with Peter Tatchell and Diane Abbott to support Hackney head teacher Jane Brown who had been suspended after refusing a charity's offer of subsidized tickets for the Royal Ballet's performance of Romeo and Juliet on the grounds that it was a "blatantly heterosexual love story".

In March, there was a meeting of the Campaign Group to discuss the situation in Bosnia, where war was raging.

"Jeremy Corbyn's position I didn't quite gather," said Tony Benn. "Bernie Grant is strongly in favour of arming the Bosnians and bombing the Serbs, and so is Lynne Jones, and the debate went backwards and forwards. The Campaign Group is always good when an issue like that crops up. We didn't reach a conclusion, but at least we had it all out and without disrupting our personal relations."

Two months later Corbyn gave one of the thirteen speeches at the funeral of Bob Cryer in Bradford. Claudia and one of their boys was there. However, later in May, he was too busy to attend the funeral of Ralph Miliband at Golders Green Crematorium in north London.

"Anyone on the real left of any significance was there," said Tony Benn.

One of the eulogist was 1960s student revolutionary Tariq Ali.

"Ralph was only seventy," said Benn. "He encouraged me in the most extraordinary way from the time the Independent Left Corresponding Society was established. Then he brought Tariq, Robin Blackburn, Perry Anderson, Hilary Wainwright, Jeremy Corbyn and me together occasionally for the Independent Left Corresponding Society, which went on until about 1992."

More rioting occurred in Oxford Street in protest again the Criminal Justice Bill that extended the police right to stop and search. It also allowed court juries to interpret a defendant's use of the right to silence and created a new offence of aggravated trespass to cover squats, unlicensed rave parties, festivals and gatherings by groups such as new age travellers.

Corbyn, who was chairing the Hyde Park rally, said: "The police deliberately charged demonstrators when they knew that everyone was leaving and a number of people were seriously hurt, including young children. The police officer in charge needs to be disciplined for his actions."

He demanded an independent enquiry into what he called the "monumentally ill-conceived" police tactics.

"Police tactics at the end set it all off," he said. "It was incompetent policing. A lower-key approach would have helped defuse the situation."

Corbyn wrote an open letter to the *Independent* about it, which was also signed by Tony Benn, Paul May and Weyman Bennett from the Coalition Against the Criminal Justice Bill. It read:

Sir: Regarding your article 'How Park Lane was turned into a battlefield' (11 October), as organisers of the national demonstration against the Criminal Justice Bill, we disagree strongly with the police statement that anarchists turned our rally into a riot. People attempting to leave the park peacefully were attacked by riot police on horses. The only group intent on organizing a riot was the Metropolitan Police, whose incompetent and aggressive policing led to a trail of violence and destruction.

Over the last few years, many demonstrations and protests have ended in a similar way, when people exercising their democratic rights to protest against Tory government policies have had to face police violence. Examples are many – the 1984/85 miners' strike, the

Wapping dispute, the poll tax and Welling demonstrations. Each time demonstrations end in violence the same old excuse is used – a minority of demonstrators caused the violence. Apparently they even planned it this time.

If this is what happens before the Criminal Justice Bill becomes law, what are we to expect when the police are given even more powers? We are demanding an inquiry into the policing of our demonstration.

In response, Janet Daley in *The Times* called Corbyn "either very naïve or very cynical" for blaming the police, while Chief Superintendent Richard Cullen accused Mr Corbyn of getting his facts wrong and "relying on the political rhetoric of the moment". He said: "My officers acted with admirable restraint. I dare say some officers retaliated. You can't expect police officers to come under such violent attacks and not retaliate."

Further violence broke out outside the Houses of Parliament when Corbyn addressed a "people's parliament rally" against the Criminal Justice Bill at Westminster Central Hall. It was called off when a firework set off a fire alarm.

The Campaign Group invited Gerry Adams to visit the House of Commons in October 1994 after an exclusion order banning him from the mainland was dropped, before the official peace process was underway.

"We are re-issuing our earlier invitation to him to come to speak to MPs to explain what the Sinn Féin demands are likely to be ahead of the negotiations with the government," Corbyn told the *Independent*.

The meeting did not go off without incident. Corbyn and Benn were escorting the Sinn Féin leader to the MPs' cafeteria when he was confronted by the young Tory turk Alan Duncan. Much to the embarrassment of his hosts, Duncan marched up and challenged Adams to express his sorrow for the murder of Airey Neave, who was blown up in the Palace of Westminster car park by Irish terrorists in 1979. Adams replied that he regretted all murders.

"Then we shook hands," says Duncan. "I just felt somebody ought to walk straight up to him, look him in the eye and confront him about these things. I only hope his handshake is worth something."

When Tony Blair took over the leadership of the Labour Party in July 1994, it was clear that he was going to suffer just as much opposition from Corbyn as Kinnock had. At the end of his speech at the 1994 Labour Party conference, Blair said that "New Labour" intended to scrap Clause IV of the party's constitution that promised: "To secure for the workers by hand or by brain the full fruits of their industry and the most equitable distribution thereof that may be possible upon the basis of the common ownership of the means of production, distribution and exchange, and the best obtainable system of popular administration and control of each industry or service."

In May 1995, Corbyn signed a letter to the *Independent* which condemned New Labour as part of the Common Ownership Campaign. It said:

Sir: The destruction of Clause IV is an attempt to change the fundamental character of the British Labour Party and accept the situation in which ownership of private capital confers overwhelming economic, social and therefore political power.

New Labour is aiming to distance itself from the trade unions, which originally established the Labour Party, and adopt a neutral stance in struggles about working conditions, impoverishment and social degradation.

It is failing to come to grips with the fact that exploitation is more rapacious than ever, and inequalities are growing in every part of our society.

Crucial as a Labour electoral victory is at the present time, we should recognise that a change of administration without a dramatic change of political direction will lead to huge disappointment among the population. We need a new, far-reaching initiative at local, national and European level to tackle mass unemployment. We should seek to promote real equality in the public services, particularly in education and the NHS, and take steps to end the tragedy of overcrowding and homelessness.

We must recreate a genuinely universal system of public welfare, capable of defending everyone from youth to old age against involuntary poverty and deprivation.

Power must be transferred outwards from the centre, and national resources must be liberated to meet the environmental, productive and domestic requirements of our people. We must pursue policies which aim to end discrimination, achieve peace, and address the vast problem of world hunger.

To work for these goals we need to remobilise the Labour and Trade Union movements, the better to create means of representing the poor, the weak, and the socially excluded, together with all those whose needs have been disregarded by Conservative governments. We need also to advance the case for democratic common ownership, and explain its relevance to these problems.

At the time, he estimated that up to a hundred Labour MPs were also "upset at the direction in which the party is being moved". He also made his views on Britain's independent nuclear deterrent perfectly clear.

"Holding nuclear weapons is expensive, immoral and unjustifiable and the only way that Britain can look the rest of the world in the eye in the year in which the Non-Proliferation Treaty is up for renegotiation is by a programme of removing all nuclear weapons and bases from this country," he told the House of Commons. To Tory amusement, Conservative Defence Secretary Malcolm Rifkind replied that the MP's views very carefully reflected those of Tony Blair – fifteen years earlier.

Corbyn was concerned that Blair was making decisions affecting the party with a small kitchen cabinet of unelected officials, after a strategy leaked to the *Guardian* had not been shown to deputy party leader John Prescott.

"I think John Prescott is being sidelined a bit," Corbyn told the *Sunday Times*. "There is a lot of concern in the party at the influence of unelected officials in the leader's office."

He was also critical of a policy document drawn up by Blair and education spokesman David Blunkett before the 1995 party conference in Brighton.

"The document is too vague," said Corbyn. "It provides the option for grant-maintained schools to continue, which is a threat to comprehensive education. It would be a two-tier system with grant-maintained schools performing the role of grammar schools. They are becoming selective. London Oratory is no exception."

Blair had recently sent his eldest son Euan to the London Oratory school rather than a local comprehensive, which angered many Labour activists.

"We should be the party of universal comprehensive education and recognise that teachers require support rather than spending on an elitist system of super-teachers," he said.

At the conference, Corbyn pushed for taking privatized industries back into public ownership. While Blair backed the Conservative bill giving automatic life sentences to convicted rapists and other violent criminals who re-offend – much to the outrage of judges – Corbyn denounced the new measures, saying: "This Tory measure runs a grave risk of being authoritarian. The idea that our leadership backs it is bad news - politicians aren't in court to hear the particulars of every single case."

Corbyn also opposed Gordon Brown's plan for saving money on child benefit.

"It has done a lot of damage to the party and we must get rid of it," he said.

Corbyn took another swipe at Murdoch in December 1995 when the Campaign Group signed up to the motion which said: "This House ... considers that News International have abused tax avoidance arrangements by amongst other complex transactions using letter-box companies in off-shore tax havens, and calls upon the Chancellor and the courts to close these loopholes."

This was just at the moment when new party leader Tony Blair was courting Murdoch.

Chapter Six – Swimming Against the Tide

With New Labour ruling the roost, it was clear that Corbyn was swimming against the tide. In 1996 he stood for the last shadow Cabinet place before the election and came bottom of the poll with thirty-seven votes. Soon after, he backed Clare Short's attack on Blair's leadership style.

"Clare is quite right to draw attention to the appalling power of the spin doctors and the way that politics is dominated by totally unrepresentative focus groups," he said. "There is a real danger of us upsetting our core support which could lose the election. It is not a question of the advisers – it is the direction in which Tony Blair is trying to take the party."

At the Labour Party conference in Blackpool in the autumn of 1996, Corbyn entered the British Airways competition that offered a Caribbean holiday for the best finish to the sentence: "I'd like to fly BA to the Caribbean because..."

The *Daily Mirror* reckoned that Corbyn had the funniest entry with: "I've promised Saddam Hussein I'll get him into the Jamaican parliament."

When the laughter subsided, Corbyn was threatened with a "yellow card" when he refused to support Blair's "Road to the Manifesto" that aimed to set New Labour up for the election. He also opposed the erection of the millennium Ferris wheel on the South Bank, when thousands were homeless. After being read the riot act by the Chief Whip, he unexpectedly pulled out of a speaking engagement with former Irish nationalist MP Bernadette McAliskey (nee Devlin) when it was reported that her daughter Roisin was facing extradition on charges connected to an IRA mortar attack on the British Army barracks in Osnabruck, Germany. Nevertheless, Corbyn visit Roisin McAliskey in jail when she was about to have a baby.

He attacked the Lords over travel perks for their wives.

"These are the last throes of the House of Lords before the abolition of hereditary peers," he said. "The fact they are contemplating such nonsense shows the need for an elected second chamber."

Then he took another swipe at Blair, signing a petition organized by the Socialist Workers Party that attacked Labour frontbenchers and condemned any attempt to weaken Labour's links with the trade unions. It said: "We protest at statements by David Blunkett and Tony Blair suggesting that Labour will not only keep the present anti-union laws but may make them tougher."

Corbyn said that he was not aware that it came from the SWP, adding: "I think people should look at the merits of the issue, which is defending the rights of people who belong to trades unions and the removal of the incredible restrictions that are imposed on unions in this country."

He invited further opprobrium from his leader in 1996 when he planned to hold a press conference in the House of Commons for

Gerry Adams, who was promoting his autobiography *Before the Dawn* in London. It was originally going to be called *Tiocfaidh Ar La* (*Our Day Will Come*), an IRA slogan. The Speakers Office had approved the event, deeming it within the guidelines for the use of Commons facilities by former MPs. But after some confusion about its nature, the House of Commons' Serjeant-at-Arms withdrew permission. Corbyn issued a statement saying that "dialogue with all parties remains essential if the peace process is to continue".

He was criticized from all sides for his decision to sponsor the conference.

"Gerry Adams is entitled to talk in the house," Corbyn said. "There is no ban. The Speaker was concerned about commercial book launches. That is not happening."

However, a meeting was still planned.

Corbyn had booked a room for Adams under rules allowing ex-MPs to use the Commons to promote books. But while Gerry Adams had been elected member for Belfast West from 1983 to 1992, he had refused to take his seat. Tory MP Terry Dicks said: "Gerry Adams is not a former MP in the true sense. If Corbyn is fixing this event, then Tony Blair should kick him out of the Labour party."

Corbyn had said that nothing would be achieved by "driving the IRA further into their bunker". Had the planned meeting gone ahead, Corbyn would have faced the threat of disciplinary action – possibly the loss of the Labour whip.

Tony Blair had dissociated himself and the Labour Party from Corbyn's action, while Chief Whip Donald Dewar said he had asked

Corbyn not to sponsor the original press conference. He said the meeting would have been "a clear breach of the spirit of the advice given to him and a defiance of the steps taken by the House authorities to stop the planned press conference".

"I wish to make it very clear that Mr Corbyn is acting on his own behalf and must take responsibility for so doing," said Dewar. "The Labour Party is not involved or associated in any way. We utterly condemn his proposed action."

Corbyn should have known better. A year earlier, he had sponsored the launch of Adams' book *Free Ireland: Towards a Lasting Peace* in the House of Commons. Speaker Betty Boothroyd stepped in amid claims the move was an abuse of Parliament. She told MPs that Westminster should not be used for "commercial purposes". Protest over the visit had been led by former-Minister Lord Tebbit, who was badly injured in the Brighton bomb blast. He challenged Adams to use the book to reveal where all the IRA bombs and bullets were hidden.

After the fracas in 1996, Shadow Northern Ireland Secretary Mo Mowlam said of Corbyn: "He does not speak for the Labour Party and we condemn his proposed action unreservedly. Gerry Adams should be concentrating his efforts on encouraging the IRA to restore its ceasefire, rather than promoting his book."

Fellow Labour MP Clive Soley, then chairman of the Northern Ireland Select Committee, had appealed earlier to Corbyn to "think again", while Tory MP Terry Dicks urged Labour to expel Corbyn because "Sinn Féin and the IRA are two sides of the same coin".

Conservative MP Sir James Spicer said: "It is particularly disgraceful that this should happen at a delicate time like this."

Naturally, Tony Benn was also involved in the altercation. Corbyn confirmed to him that officials had banned the press conference on the grounds that you could not use the House of Commons for promoting a commercial publication.

"Fair enough," said Benn. "So Jeremy transferred the press conference to the Irish Centre in Islington and said we'd have a meeting with Gerry Adams in the House at nine o'clock in the morning."

According to Benn, all hell then broke loose. On the one o'clock news, it was the top item. At two, Donald Dewar issued a statement saying that disciplinary action would be taken against Jeremy Corbyn.

Benn called Dewar and said: "Just to let you know I'm going to be there tomorrow."

That took him aback, said Benn. He went on: "I don't know what disciplinary action can be taken for meeting someone in the House of Commons. Ceausescu, Khrushchev and Bulganin were all there. Anyway, Gerry Adams has already met President Clinton, Vice-President Gore, Senator Bob Dole, Ted Kennedy, Nelson Mandela, and [Irish Taoiseach] John Bruton."

This took him even further aback, said Benn. The news said that the Chip Whip would move a resolution to have the whip withdrawn from Corbyn and Benn. He phoned Dewar again and said: "I'm told by *The Times* that the spin doctors are saying that you decided to move a resolution to withdraw the whip."

Then Dewar got really worried, said Benn, who told him that he would be issuing a press statement saying that he and Corbyn were searching for peace, and would be writing to Clinton, Major and Bruton, asking them if they could help to get the peace process on its way, and also to call a round-table conference on the basis of a permanent ceasefire.

The withdrawal of the whip from Corbyn and Benn was still a major item on the six o'clock news.

"Blair should have said nothing about it," said Benn. " 'It's a private initiative, nothing to do with me.' But he chose to make an issue of it and it's now being described as a test of his leadership. I have to be clear in my mind that I have taken a considerable risk, and Jeremy has too, but he's much weaker than me because to pick him out would be easier.

"All in all, it was quite a day. The phone has rung absolutely continuously, but if anything it's somewhat stiffened my resolve. I wish I hadn't got into this, because I don't want a confrontation with anybody. It did frighten me in a deep way, and Jeremy said that the ITN were camping outside his house."

While Adams had refused to take his seat at Westminster, he pointed out that he had spoken to Labour and Conservative MPs at Westminster in the past.

"My engagement is with Jeremy Corbyn," he said. "I will be there in the House of Commons. I understand, for reasons that I am not entirely au fait with, that the press conference has been proscribed."

As the controversy rumbled on, Corbyn was defended by his party colleague David Winnick MP, who was vice-chairman of the British-Irish Parliamentary body. Winnick said: "I support his right to hold the meeting but would urge him to engage in tough talking as the prospect of a united Ireland is even more remote than at any time in the past twenty-five years."

The following day, Gerry Adams called off the meeting and the papers were full of the story of "Blair's fury", which Benn thought had been put out by Peter Mandelson.

Clare Short MP, the Shadow Minister for Overseas Development, rang Corbyn and said: "I know I'm not your favourite person."

"That's right," Corbyn replied.

"I just want to say how much I support you," said Short.

Corbyn later told the *Daily Mirror* that he could not believe the fuss.

"If there's to be a peace process, clearly it has got to involve Sinn Féin and Gerry Adams," he said.

And it did; Jeremy Corbyn and Ken Livingstone did meet Sinn Féin leaders in the House of Commons. When it was leaked that they were meeting the IRA's Army Council – which Livingstone denies – there was an understandable furore. What they could not say at the time was that, despite the public protests, they were conveying messages from the Shadow Secretary of State for Northern Ireland

Mo Mowlam in the run up to the Good Friday Agreement, which she saw signed as Secretary of State in 1998.

Even so, Labour Chief Whip Donald Dewar did summon Corbyn and Livingstone to a meeting to discuss the alleged security breach after concerns were raised. Shadow Home Secretary Jack Straw said: "We take any complaints, or representations, about breaches of security very seriously indeed."

House of Commons' Speaker Betty Boothroyd was asked to investigate reports that 'top IRA men' were invited into Parliament by Labour MPs – and that one of them was left unattended there. Leader of the House Tony Newton asked her to look into claims that Sinn Féin members, who belonged to the IRA's ruling Army Council, were the guests of Labour MPs and that one of the men was allegedly allowed to go to the lavatory unaccompanied for twenty minutes, in a security lapse which breached Commons rules.

Prime Minister John Major, who had also had secret talks with Sinn Féin resulting in the 1994 cease-fire, attacked "the stunning naivety" of MPs who did not realize the connection between Sinn Féin and the IRA.

Livingstone said the Sinn Féin members he had met were not among known members of the IRA Army Council. He poured scorn on the idea that members of the army council would come to London "to case the joint for bomb runs".

He said about seven Labour MPs had met Mitchel McLaughlin, chairman of Sinn Féin in Northern Ireland, some three weeks earlier, because Mr McLaughlin wanted to "see what the current thinking was about the ceasefire".

"It's like the bad old days of the mid-70s with people inside MI5 living in a fantasy world of their own," said Livingstone. "No wonder the IRA keep on getting away with so much if that's the competence of MI5's detective work."

He also pointed out that anybody could walk into the House of Commons, particularly the central lobby, which was where they met the Sinn Féin representatives.

Chapter Seven – Not New Labour

In the run-up to the election in 1997, New Labour tried to silence its critics. That January 1997, there was a meeting of the Parliamentary Labour Party to discuss the new Standing Orders. The nub of them was that you could be suspended from the Party or have the whip withdrawn "for action likely to bring the Party into disrepute". Corbyn managed to thwart this with an amendment though.

The following month, Corbyn and Benn attended an international conference against the Maastricht Treaty at Central Hall, Westminster. They had defied the party whips, voting against the bill in the House of Commons. At the conference, people from eighteen nations were represented. They came from all over Europe – France, Germany, Italy – even Brazil.

"It was a marvellous rally and the great thing about it was that it was international," Benn noted in his diaries. "Nobody could say that this was the British against Europe. This was the European working class against the bankers and the Commissioners. There was an item on the six o'clock news quoting 'the two MPs' (Jeremy Corbyn and me) were totally unrepresentative of the Party."

Despite his staunch opposition to Tony Blair and New Labour, Corbyn was re-elected in May with 24,834 votes, a majority of 19,955, increasing his lead, yet again – this time by 11.9 percent.

Analysing the results in the *Independent*, Polly Toybee asked: "What's Jeremy Corbyn doing in the same party as Tony Blair?"

According to Matthew Parris in *The Times*, Corbyn was "loathed by the leadership of his party". He said: "The new Minister for Sport, Tony Banks, was seen to be crossing his fingers while taking the Oath (Banks is a republican and vehemently opposed to the monarchy), most people just laughed it off. That is because we do not choose to make an issue of this with Mr Banks, who is rather popular in London. If Jeremy Corbyn, a less charismatic leftie, ... were to have told the news media that he would hold up crossed fingers for the TV cameras while taking the Oath, and if there were to be a fuss about this at Westminster, he might well have been disbarred."

Of course Corbyn is a republican, but he believed abolition of the monarchy could wait, because his priority was "social justice".

Following Labour's election victory in 1997, Corbyn did not stay in waiting for a call from Tony Blair. He was hardly likely to be offered a job in government. He knew he was not popular with his new boss – so to provoke him further, Corbyn, an ardent republican, petitioned Blair to evict the Royal Family from Buckingham Palace and move them into "more modest" accommodation.

When Blair first became party leader in 1994, Corbyn had taken a stronger line.

"A referendum on scrapping the monarchy should be in our next manifesto - it would be very popular," he said.

Once New Labour were in power, his next target was Peter Mandelson over his fund-raising plans for the Millennium Dome, which stood to make promoter Mark McCormack £9 million.

"I am appalled that the Millennium Commission should be following the Tory tradition of giving money to fat cats who appear to need carrots to work," he said. "A Labour government should be promoting a popular celebration of the millennium and dealing with the special needs of this country rather than lining the pockets of Mr McCormack and his ilk."

Then he piled the agony on Tony Blair for taking money from Bernie Ecclestone, Blair's first major embarrassment since taking office.

"Tobacco advertising on Formula One cars encourages boys to smoke and end up dying early. It's as simple as that," he said. "If we mean what we say about tobacco bans, we should apply it to Formula One. There has been a major change in policy on a very important health issue. The issue is why the Government decided to do this complete about-turn under an alleged threat that Formula One would move out of Britain. We can't be held to ransom because Bernie Ecclestone says some of his supporters might move away."

Labour was forced to repay the £1-million Ecclestone had donated to party funds.

In July 1997, Corbyn joined Benn, Livingstone, Skinner and others abstaining in a vote to continue rate capping councils, condemning it as "an infringement of local democracy".

As a vegetarian, Corbyn took an active interest in the "McLibel trial" that had just ended. Starting in June 1994, it had become the longest civil case in British history. In 1986, London Greenpeace, a small environmental campaigning group, put together a six-page pamphlet called *What's Wrong With McDonald's? – Everything they don't want you to know.* It said the quest for cash crops by multi-national companies, such as McDonald's, caused starvation in the Third World. They were responsible for damage to the environment, including destruction of rain forests. McDonald's packaging was wasteful and harmful. Their food with its low fibre and high fat, sodium and sugar content were linked to medical conditions including heart disease and cancer. Their advertising exploited children. The cattle were reared and slaughtered in a barbaric fashion. The campaigners pointed out the lousy conditions that workers in the food service industry suffered, the low wages paid by McDonald's and the company's hostility to trades unions.

The pamphlet was still being distributed in 1990 when McDonald's started a libel action against the supporters of London Greenpeace. Three of those named chose to apologize. Vegetarians Helen Steel and Dave Morris would not and the case went to court.

Giving his verdict on 19 June 1997, the judge, Mr Justice Bell, found that McDonald's published unjustified, defamatory statements about the defendants in an attempt to discredit them, but said this was permissible in law, ruling that the company had the right to self-defence. He awarded McDonald's £60,000, though their legal cost greatly exceeded that and, in any case, the defendants could not afford to pay it.

Once the judge's 17 July deadline for any further applications had passed, Corbyn sponsored two early day motions to be put before parliament, referring to Mr Justice Bell's findings in the trial and slamming the McDonald's Corporation over its "deceptive and exploitative business practices". They also called for "effective sanctions" against the company, who should pay "appropriate compensation". The early day motions further condemn "unfair and oppressive libel laws" and call for "urgent reform to safeguard public rights".

An appeal began on 12 January 1999. The three Appeal Court judges were sympathetic to the defendants, but still found for McDonald's – though they reduced the damages by £20,000. Steel and Morris then went to the European Court of Human Rights who found they had been denied a fair trial and deprived of their right to freedom of expression. The UK government were ordered to pay £57,000 in compensation.

Corbyn, Benn, Tam Dalyell and other prominent left-wingers joined forces again in November 1997 when David Winnick put a private notice question on the situation in Iraq. Winnick was condemned as an "absolute franatic".

"The public are not at all keen on another war with Iraq," said Benn, "yet Blair is making the most militant statements and the media are full of pictures of Tornado fighters and Cruise missiles and God knows what."

A few days later Corbyn and the Campaign Group threatened to vote against the government over cuts to single-parent family benefits. In the streets, Corbyn aligned himself with students on a march to oppose the cutting of grants and the imposition of university fees.

"We have to address the problems of society by redistributing wealth," Corbyn told a rally in Hyde Park. "F*** the rich."

Or, at least, that was how *The Times* reported it on 27 November. Five days later, they published a correction saying: "He should have been reported as saying 'tax the rich.'"

In January 1998, Corbyn asked Benn to support him in the Nobel Peace Prize nomination of Mordecai Vanunu, the Israeli scientist held in solitary confinement in Shikma Prison after telling the *Sunday Times* that Israel had nuclear weapons. When Corbyn flew out to Israel, the government denied him access to Vanunu and his continued efforts to visit him became an embarrassment to Tony Blair.

Corbyn turned out again at a rally protesting against a vote in the House of Commons approving the bombing of Iraq organized by George Galloway on 18 February 1998.

Benn wrote: "I went to Whitehall for one of these vigils outside Downing Street and it was huge, bigger than last Saturday's. It was candlelit, very moving. Marion Miliband was there, Tariq Ali, Harold Pinter, a well-known actress whose name I have forgotten, Jeremy Corbyn and George Galloway. We made speeches and did lots of interviews and then went and presented a letter. Three guys tried to manacle themselves to the gates of Downing Street."

In the eyes of New Labour, Corbyn was now a fully paid-up member of the awkward squad, along with Ken Livingstone and Dennis Skinner – what Blair called "the usual suspects" who opposed the government at every turn. As a result, "on a vote of 14 to two – with Dennis Skinner and Ken Livingstone once again the sole dissenting voices – the NEC has given the party high command two new powers," said the *Guardian* on 28 May. "First, the whips will now be authorized to send reports on sitting MPs to their constituency parties, detailing their voting record and parliamentary conduct. The assumption is that members of the Awkward Squad – the likes of Tony Benn, Diane Abbott, Jeremy Corbyn, Alan Simpson, Bob Marshall-Andrews as well as Messrs Skinner and Livingstone – will be the subject of thorough indictments despatched from the whips' office and all but inviting their local parties to kick them out in favour of someone more reliable. All votes against the Government, as well as any 'unauthorized absences', will be marked down and recorded – ready for inclusion in the final, dreaded charge sheet."

The newspaper then helpfully added: "If absenteeism is a crime , then Sedgefield should be alerted: Tony Blair has one of the worst attendance records in the Commons."

It seemed that Corbyn took no notice. On 5 June, the *Daily Mirror* reported that he was one of ten Labour MPs who had been threatened with a "yellow card" over their voting record in the

Commons. He was, the paper added, "a law unto himself," according to a Westminster insider.

Corbyn found himself on the side of the government, momentarily, in October 1998 when General Augusto Pinochet, the former dictator of Chile, came to London on a shopping trip and was arrested, after being indicted by a Spanish magistrate for human rights violations. The fascist dictatorship of Pinochet had long been an issue for Corbyn. In 1973, the general had seized power in his native country in a CIA-backed coup that overthrew the Socialist President Salvador Allende, resulting in Allende's death.

Corbyn said that Allende was the historical figure he most identified with.

"I think he was a very interesting guy in many ways," he said. "Very thoughtful, deep man."

Asked if he had ever met him, he said: "I've met many people in Chile but unfortunately not him. He was brought down by the CIA, with the help of the British."

Determined to crush the opposition, Pinochet's regime had arrested 130,000, many of whom were tortured, in its first three years alone. Pinochet stayed in office until 1990. A report of the National Commission for Truth and Reconciliation determined that under his government 2,279 people were killed for political reasons, including 957 who "disappeared" after arrest and 164 "victims of political violence". Another report found that over 30,000 people had been tortured for political reasons.

Corbyn had taken a consistent line over Pinochet. After all, his wife was Chilean. During an earlier visit in 1994, Corbyn said he would be taking the matter up with the foreign secretary.

"I shall be asking how it is that such a man was allowed to visit Britain, and how much money was spent on his protection," he told the *Independent*. "He is the second most evil man of the century, after Hitler. He is responsible for the deaths of 50,000 civilians."

Although by 1998 Chile had a civil government, Pinochet remained head of the armed forces and was visiting Britain to discuss buying "Rayo", a planned multiple-launch rocket system which, BAe said was a deal of "certainly millions, and potentially tens of millions of pounds".

That was not good enough.

"It is time we started using the skills of arms manufacturing workers to make civilian goods," said Corbyn. "We'll never be able to be critical of human rights violations around the world if we have to sell arms to these countries all the time."

He also condemned the "blood trade" in arms to Indonesia. Genocide had been committed in its occupation of East Timor where 200,000 people had been killed and two British-made Hawk aircraft had been used on a bombing mission there, he said.

When Pinochet stepped down as president, he was given immunity from prosecution in Chile. However, some of those who had been tortured were Spanish citizens and the Spanish authorities sought to have Pinochet extradited from the UK. Once more, Corbyn campaigned for Pinochet's prosecution.

"The fact that one of the great murderers of this century was entertained by Lady Thatcher confirms everything I have always believed about her support for Pinochet," said Corbyn, then leading the campaign against the general. "She maintained trade links and effectively prevented any investigation into human rights violations."

As vice-chair of the All-Party Parliamentary Human Rights Group, Corbyn signed an open letter to *The Times* saying:

Sir, Whatever General Pinochet's motives for giving assistance to the UK during the Falklands war, the fact remains that thousands of innocent people were tortured, murdered and disappeared under his Government. The human rights abuses he inflicted from 1973 outweigh any other consideration.

Prior to the Argentine conflict, Chile had been on the point of war against Argentina over a border dispute. Certainly, his assistance to the UK in this instance did him no harm. His alleged selfless help for the British contrasts sharply, however, with the treatment of British citizens such as William Beausire and Sheila Cassidy, only two of the many victims of the human rights violations committed under his regime.

If the Spanish extradition fails, the British Government has an obligation under the United Nations Convention Against Torture and Other Cruel, Inhuman or Degrading Treatment or Punishment. Under Article 6 any state is obliged to take into custody or take other legal measures to ensure the presence of any person within its territory who has been alleged to have committed torture. The Government is also obliged under international law to co-operate with the Spanish judicial authorities under the European Convention on the Suppression of Terrorism.

The arrest of General Pinochet is a positive step in obtaining justice for the victims of his regime. The British Government should actively consider the possibilities of prosecuting him in this country in order to obtain justice for the many thousands of victims and their families, a view that we know is shared by more than forty of our colleagues.

If the International Criminal Court were up and running, and also retrospective, the case of General Pinochet would be referred to it. Now that the Government has put human rights at the front of its foreign policy, what better opportunity to demonstrate this commitment?

The Law Lords voted three to two that Pinochet, who was then in hospital, did not have immunity from prosecution in other countries as a former head of state. This was hailed by Corbyn as a "great day for justice". Torture victim Sheila Cassidy, who had been tied, naked to a metal bed and subjected to repeated electric shocks by Pinochet's police, said the verdict made her "proud to be British".

"There are really no grounds for compassion," said Corbyn. "He came here to buy arms. He had a very minor back operation in a private hospital. He is a man who had perpetrated crimes against humanity and has not shown the slightest bit of remorse."

When Home Secretary Jack Straw decided that the extradition should go ahead, Corbyn was an enthusiastic supporter.

"Jack Straw has made a correct, courageous and brilliant decision that coincides with the fiftieth anniversary of the Universal Declaration of Human Rights," he said.

However, when it was discovered that Lord Hoffmann, one of the Law Lords, had failed to declare in advance his relationship with Amnesty International, the matter had to be considered again. Corbyn then submitted a petition signed by over 850,000 to deny Pinochet's plea of immunity.

"The overwhelming weight of popular democratic opinion all over the world says this international terrorist must be brought to justice," he said.

Not everyone saw it that way. Corbyn received death threats. Posters put up in his Islington constituency read: "3,000 missing. Jeremy Corbyn MP, you're next." The posters gave the address of Internet sites of gun-toting US extremists.

On second vote by the Law Lords, Pinochet lost again – this time six to one. Nevertheless, he was eventually allowed to return to Chile in January 2000 after a British court ruled that he was physically unfit to stand trial.

However, the furore stirred up by Corbyn and others galvanized human-rights organizations in Chile. The US and other countries released formerly classified documents concerning the "disappeared" and Pinochet was stripped of his immunity from prosecution. The first prosecutions failed when Chile's Supreme Court ruled that he was mentally incapable of defending himself.

More cases were outstanding, including those concerning gun-running and drug-trafficking. On his 91st birthday he issued a statement saying: "I assume the political responsibility for all that has been done."

Two days later he was sentenced to house arrest for the kidnapping and murder of Salvador Allende's bodyguards. Two weeks after that, Pinochet died.

Corbyn went on campaigning. During the 1999 Defence Systems Equipment International show in Chertsey, Surrey, he joined a demonstration against the arms trade, telling protesters: "Visitors are coming here to buy weapons that will be used to kill people at some time somewhere in the world. There is no point in condemning human rights abuses around the world if we are selling weapons which the death squads are using."

He was back with the awkward squad. In June 1999, when the Kosovo crisis was at its climax and NATO began bombing military targets in Serbia, Corbyn and Benn walked over to 10 Downing Street to deliver a letter about the situation. They voted against intervention. Clare Short, then International Development Secretary, declared the rebels to be a "disgrace to the Labour Party".

Corbyn took his anti-war stance to its logical conclusion. He went on to propose that pacifists should not be forced to pay the part of their taxes which would be spent on the armed forces.

"British taxpayers have a right of conscience not to be in the armed forces in time of war," he told the House of Commons. "Why shouldn't they have the same right in time of peace?"

Chapter Eight – A Matter of Principle

Jeremy Corbyn and his second wife Claudia were together for twelve years and had three sons. But they divorced in 1999, after she refused to send Benjamin, the second of their sons to a failing comprehensive school.

"I had to make the decision as a mother and a parent," said Claudia. "I had no choice."

Corbyn said that he felt "very strongly about comprehensive education" and could not agree to send his son to a grammar school – so much so that he moved out of their family home and into a flat in nearby.

"I would never have sent my son to anywhere but a state school. I would not have followed Tony Blair's example," he said. Blair had snubbed comprehensive schools near his home in Islington, north London, to send his sons to the London Oratory, a grant-maintained boys-only Roman Catholic school in Fulham.

Again, for Corbyn, this was a private matter and he objected to the media intrusion into his private life.

"I hated that period. I hated the publicity for it. I hated the pressure put on my kids as a result of it, and it was very unpleasant and very intrusive," he said. "We divorced. We have three kids; we get on very well; we talk to each other; and I don't like dragging personal things into my political life. And I think it's very sad when that happens. I don't criticise anybody else for what happens with their children, and I don't expect people to interfere with my children's lives."

As with Jane Chapman, Corbyn said that he continued to "get on very well" with his ex-wife, though Ben was later sent to Queen Elizabeth's School, which was Claudia's first choice. She explained: "My children's education is my absolute priority and this situation left me with no alternative but to accept a place at Queen Elizabeth Boys' School. This decision was made by myself alone and without the consent of my husband. The difficulties of making decisions under these circumstances have played an important role in bringing about a regrettable marital break-up."

But her reasons were clear and irrevocable.

"I could not compromise my son's future for my husband's career," she said. "I regret it is going to be difficult for Jeremy but it was an impossible decision. Nobody really is a winner."

Corbyn was equally adamant.

"My views on selective education are very important to me," he said. "It's gone, it's past and people should leave personal stuff out of it if they can … I've got three boys and love them dearly and we get along great."

However, Corbyn's brother Piers said that there was more to it than that, hinting that Jeremy may have been unfaithful.

"Something like that must have been going on when they finally split up but I don't know who was bad first," Piers told *The Sun On Sunday*.

He claimed the couple split up before their row over schooling, saying they had "fallen out of love with each other after finding attractions elsewhere".

At the time his twelve-year marriage collapsed Corbyn insisted: "I'm certainly not involved with anybody else at the moment."

He certainly did not want the matter aired in public.

"Claudia and I have been separated for two years," he said in May 1999. "I have not sought to make this public because I believe it to be a private matter. Unfortunately, the issue of our eldest son's education has brought it to public attention. Our separation is amicable and my wife retains primary care of the children. I maintain the closest possible relationship with my three children and intend to continue to do so."

By then, Corbyn, though divorced, had moved back in with his wife for the sake of the children. They had moved into a new house that was large enough to divide in two. Builders transformed the top two floors into a home for Claudia and the boys while Jeremy lived in the basement.

"I hope it will work out, but we're very much in the early stages of being separated but under the same roof," she said.

They were also politically active together. Jeremy, Claudia and the three boys all appeared together on the platform on the "Stop the War" march in February 2003, along with Jesse Jackson, Bianca

Jagger and Ken Loach. His eldest son Ben became a football coach. Seb went on to work for John McDonnell MP and Tommy was an electronics student at university.

Corbyn's life-long commitment to Socialism never faltered. In May 2000, Corbyn spoke in a debate about it in the new chamber in Westminster Hall. He was also a football fan – a supporter of Arsenal, whose Emirates Stadium lies at the heart of his constituency. In July 2000, he voted against the second reading of the Football (Disorder) Bill, which gave the police the power to stop suspected soccer hooligans travelling abroad. Bank in February 1987, he had signed a motion called "Crisis in London Football" introduced by Tony Banks, ruing the proposed merger of Fulham and Queen's Park Rangers.

In 1995, he had also gone out to bat for cricket. Taking its cue from Kick Racism Out Of Football, cricket fans had started Hit Racism for Six in 1995. At the launch Corbyn said: "I welcome the fact that black players are in the England team. If one is able to break through the sickening racism so apparent on the English cricket ground, then one must have a hell of a motivated player."

He also showed an occasional flash of wit in the House. During an all-night sitting, he said to Tory MP Quentin Davies: "You obviously practise megaphone diplomacy. Will you stop shouting? It is very disturbing to many of us up here who are trying to rest."

In January 2001, Corbyn took up the two-thousand Indian Ocean islanders – the Ilois – who had been thrown out of the Chagos Islands in the 1960s to make way for construction of the US military base on Diego Garcia in exchange for £5 million off the cost of a joint UK/US missile programme. He called on the government to apologize to the islanders.

"I hope the government is prepared to settle a compensation claim, rather than just the costs of the return of the people of the islands," he added.

The islanders and their offspring were granted British citizenship in 2002.

"These people have lived in terrible poverty in exile," said Corbyn. "They have been very badly treated by Britain. Granting them citizenship is a promising move, but it does not give them the right of return."

The battle for their return still rages on.

In February 2001, he accused the Government of being America's poodle in their "gung-ho" air attacks on Baghdad. He said: "It is extremely dangerous and the public reaction is pretty hostile. Within the Labour Party the reaction is extremely hostile."

He also called for the bombing of Afghanistan, after the 9/11 attacks, be halted as it "seems to be directed in part against conscripted soldiers and civilian targets". Its objectives, he said, were unclear. Blair insisted that there were "no civilian targets at all" in Afghanistan.

Ten days after the attacks on the World Trade Center and the Pentagon, Corbyn was elected as the National Chair of the Stop the War Coalition, which helped to mobilize opposition to the

Afghanistan War. Meanwhile, Blair swung his weight behind George W. Bush.

That year Corbyn also won the Beard of the Year contest – narrowly beating Rolf Harris – after having described his beard as a form of dissent against New Labour. The previous year, Frank Dobson was named "Beard 2000", amid controversy over his claim that Labour spin doctors had told him to shave off his prize-winning beard for the upcoming elections for Mayor of London, which he lost to Ken Livingstone running as an independent. Dobson said that he had told them to "Stick it up their wicket". Corbyn has won the coveted "Parliamentary Beard of Year" award five times. Other title holders have included Robin Cook, George Galloway and David Blunkett.

By this time, Corbyn was so out of favour with New Labour that, when a notebook was mislaid by a member of the Whips' Office in 2002, he was reportedly described in it as "Jeremy Cor Bin-Laden".

He outraged monarchists once more when he wore a bright red blazer in the House of Commons during eulogies to the Queen Mother in March 2002. Later, when his house was burgled, the blazer was thrown out of the window of the getaway car as the thieves made off with their meagre swag.

He took another pop at the monarchy at the state opening of parliament in November 2002; Corbyn said: "We should start behaving like a modern Parliamentary democracy, not a Ruritanian nation stuck in the eighteenth century."

Corbyn's opposition to the government resumed its serious tone during the build up to the invasion of Iraq in 2003. He spoke out against it in the House of Commons and at dozens of anti-war rallies in Britain and overseas.

On 15 February 2003 he played a key role in organizing what is widely regarded as the biggest political protest event in British history, when over one million people marched against the Iraq War. There were cheers at the Labour Party conference in October when he asked: "Why are we, a British Labour Government with a very large parliamentary majority so signed up to the ultra right- wing George Bush?"

At the Annual General Meeting of the "Stop the War" campaign in the Camden Centre, in February 2004, Tony Benn said that Corbyn made a "brilliant speech". The veteran campaigner said: "Jeremy is so thoughtful and experienced and clear."

A few weeks later, they were together again in Trafalgar Square with Julie Christie, Corin Redgrave, Bruce Kent and a couple of thousand other people for a CND protest.

There was still fun and games to be had. In May 2004, he seconded fellow London Labour backbencher Tony Banks' "Pigeon Bomb" early day motion that said: "That this House is appalled, but barely surprised, at the revelations in M15 files regarding the bizarre and inhumane proposals to use pigeons as flying bombs; recognises the important and live-saving role of carrier pigeons in two world wars and wonders at the lack of gratitude towards these gentle creatures; and believes that humans represent the most obscene, perverted, cruel, uncivilized and lethal species ever to inhabit the planet and looks forward to the day when the inevitable asteroid slams into the earth and wipes them out thus giving nature the opportunity to start again."

There was only one other backer, but Conservative MP Peter Bottomley had fun proposing amendments.

On 29 September 2004, Special Branch phoned Corbyn. It was thought that, because of his anti-war credentials that he might be able to help out in the case of Ken Bigley, the British civil engineer who had been kidnapped in Baghdad by al-Qaeda in Iraq. Corbyn had already pledged to raise Bigley's fate at the Labour Party conference in Brighton.

There he chaired an anti-war meeting where Ken Bigley's brother Paul said: "I do not look for Tony Blair's head on the block like my brother's could be. I do not like Tony Blair's policies. But if he continues with his policies he should be removed from office."

It did no good. Bigley was beheaded by his captors on 7 October. The "Stop the War" campaign were then accused of supporting the killers after it drew up a draft statement saying the Iraqi people should use "whatever means they find necessary" to end the occupation by coalition forces. Corbyn was one of those who struck back, saying: "The violence in Iraq during the invasion and since the occupation by the USA and Britain has cost the lives of US, British, other coalition and Iraqi service people and an uncounted number of Iraqi civilians." Much of the unacceptable violence in Iraq was the result of the occupation and he called for a "timetabled withdrawal" of British forces.

Unapologetic Corbyn turned out at a "Stop the War" peace demonstration in Trafalgar Square alongside Che Guevara's daughter. Tony Benn said there were "at least 100,000" people there, "but the police said 20,000. Why they can't count, I don't know."

Corbyn drew more praise from Tony Benn at a "Hands off Venezuela" conference in December 2005.

"He is such a brilliant man," said Benn, who was also speaking. "He's known Latin America for thirty years."

A week later they turned out again together for an International Peace Conference, called by the Stop the War Coalition.

The following month they had to attend the funeral of Tony Bank's at the City of London Crematorium along with Chris Mullin, Diane Abbott, Tessa Jowell, Margaret Beckett, John Prescott, Alastair Campbell and David Mellor, who gave a "perfectly good and amusing speech".

"Tony's body was brought into the chapel in a wicker coffin," said Benn. "The music was lovely."

Naturally, Corbyn, Benn and Abbott had lunch with Hugo Chávez when Ken Livingston invited him to London's City Hall. Later they went to the House of Commons where Chávez was speaking in the Churchill Room.

"Afterwards we had another photograph with him," said Benn, "and I talked to Jeremy Corbyn, who knows Venezuela well, and the Campaign Group crowded round."

Corbyn and Benn were also patrons of the Palestine Solidarity Committee together.

In March 2006, Corbyn showed his opposition to New Labour at a protest meeting in Parliament Square where the twenty-eight war crimes charges against the governments of Tony Blair and George Bush were read out. The charges claimed that Britain is a signatory to the Geneva and Hague conventions and the Nuremberg charter of 1945, but had breached them all during the Iraq war in 2003 and its aftermath. The use of white phosphorus as a weapon in the assault on Fallujah was also cited as a war crime. This was initially denied by the Bush administration, until US troops boasted on a website that it had been used to flush out insurgents. The charge sheet included the use of cable ties as a restraint; hooding of detainees which caused mental suffering; the use of dogs as a means of obtaining information, which was authorized by the US Defence Secretary, Donald Rumsfeld, in December 2002; the sexual humiliation of detainees, including rapes; and the use of cluster bombs and depleted uranium shells.

The indictments included: crimes against peace; planning and conducting an aggressive war using deceit; failure to ensure public order and safety by disbanding the army and police of Iraq; extensive destruction of service infrastructure; deliberate damage to hospitals; failure to prohibit looting and arson; failure to respect cultural property; and economic exploitation of occupied territories. These were sent to UN Secretary General Kofi Annan.

Later Corbyn was asked on *Newsnight* whether Blair would ever be charged with war crimes over the Iraq War.

"Is he going to be charged for it? I don't know," said Corbyn. "Could he be tried for it? Possibly... I want to see all those that committed war crimes tried for it and those that made the decisions that went with it."

In August, he turned out a Golders Green Crematorium for the funeral of Paul Foot with Michael Foot, Richard Ingrams, Arthur Scargill et al.

"There was a lot of laughter," said Tony Benn, "so obviously there was a lot of fun, and they played Michael Flanders and Donald Swann's 'I'm a Gnu'. I don't know why they played it, but it was very funny."

Occasionally, Corbyn found himself with the mainstream. With 411 other MPs he signed the Micheal Meacher's early day motion that said: "That this House agrees with the Government's Chief Scientific Adviser that climate change is a threat to civilisation; welcomes the cross-party agreement in favour of major cuts in greenhouse gas emissions, and particularly in carbon dioxide emissions, by 2050; believes that such a long-term target will best be met through a series of more regular milestones; and therefore notes the Climate Change Bill that was presented by a cross-party group of honourable Members in the final days before the General Election, and hopes that such a Bill will be brought forward in this Parliament so that annual cuts in carbon dioxide emissions of 3 percent can be delivered in a framework that includes regular reporting and new scrutiny and corrective processes."

Here he found himself at odds with his brother.

In 2006, Corbyn announced that he might run for the position of deputy leader Labour Party, but decided against it. The race was won by Harriet Harman. But on 31 October 2006, Mr Corbyn was one of twelve Labour MPs to back Plaid Cymru and the Scottish National Party's call for an inquiry into the war.

The question was later put: Corbyn seemed so distant from New Labour, had he ever considered leaving the party?

"I've often been extremely frustrated by the Labour party, particularly over Iraq and, earlier, on Vietnam," he replied. "Then you think what the Labour party has achieved, and that it is the electoral home to millions of people, so I'm still in it. Always have been. I remember discussing this with Tony Benn many times, and he said: 'You know, comrade, we're just in it, aren't we?' Tony was a very close friend."

Chapter Nine – The Brown Years

Finally, in June 2007, Tony Blair stood down and Gordon Brown took over as leader of the party and prime minister. Although the left considered Brown a good guy, unlike his predecessor, Corbyn continued to appear on every list of rebels. Asked by a *Guardian* reporter if he thought Brown had an ideology and, if so, could he describe it, Corbyn just smiled. No, he said, he didn't think Gordon had an ideology; or if he had, it would take many paragraphs to explain.

Brown's response was to refuse Corbyn entry to Downing Street when he and Tony Benn were trying to deliver a letter calling for troops to be pulled out of Afghanistan.

"It's a shabby way of treating the majority of British people who are alarmed by the loss of life in Afghanistan," Corbyn said.

He attacked Brown for appointing Lord Digby Jones, who was not a member of the Labour Party, the position of trade and investment minister. When the former CBI chief spoke up against charging non-doms £30,000 a year, Corbyn said: "This is the danger of having non-Labour people in a Labour government. Non-doms have been evading tax for a very long time. The decision to close the loophole was a very welcome one."

Corbyn then found himself on a secret blacklist of Labour MPs suspected to be plotting to defeat Gordon Brown's flagship terror reforms in April 2008. He voted against the bill, but it passed with a majority of just nine votes.

He called for former sports minister Kate Hoey to be expelled from the Labour Party after she agreed to work for Boris Johnson if he became Mayor of London. Corbyn said she had broken party rules.

"She should get behind Ken Livingstone," he told Channel 4 News: "Labour Party rules say that you are not supposed to do anything to support a candidate who is standing against an official Labour candidate."

But when Harriet Harman raised the issue of social class and Gordon Brown promised to "adapt and rethink New Labour policy", Corbyn was full of praise.

"At long last they've started to read the runes and realize that the biggest fall in support for Labour is among the traditional working class," he said. "We've been losing the core Labour vote and we can't win without them. Maybe this is an attempt to reconnect with them."

Nevertheless, Gordon Brown had to fight off a total of 103 revolts during the 2007-08 parliamentary session. This was the most inflicted on any governing party for more than thirty years, with Corbyn still being listed as the most rebellious MP. He revolted on 57 occasions in 2007-08, compared with 31 the year before and 60 the year before that. One Union leader said that Corbyn had been "cheerfully disloyal" to all the Labour leaders he had served under.

After the 2008 banking crisis, he joined Tory MP David Davies in the early day motion: "That this House believes that all banks which have received public funds and in which the British taxpayer now owns more than fifty percent of their value should be governed by the same freedom of information rules as Parliament, and calls on the senior management of these part-nationalized banks to publish their receipts for expenses in full."

Nothing was done. Then came the MPs expenses scandal of 2009. Corbyn was squeaky clean. In terms of his expenses, he ranked 539th out of 645 MPs. His house off the Holloway Road was, he said, "my first home, my second home, my third home, my fourth home."

Although Corbyn always made it a point of pride not to brief against his parliamentary colleagues, he was once asked: "Why do you have bars in the Commons? Nobody else has bars in their place of work."

According to the *Guardian*, Corbyn "made some affable reply, which included parliament's up-itself tradition of referring to drunks on the benches as honourable gentleman who have 'lunched too well'."

During one accounting period, it was reported that he had the lowest claim in the Commons – £8.95 for a printer cartridge. When he was questioned about this he said he would like to come clean – he had screwed up his expenses.

"You had to pay within a certain period for things, and somewhere along the line we claimed for one print cartridge, but the rest of the stuff was slightly slower going in so that went into the next claim period, which was a much more realistic claim," he said. A more typical Corbyn claim might run to "a few hundred quid each quarter".

"There were no bills I needed to claim for during this three-month period but in the next claim period, my office rent and various office costs will feature," he said. "I am a parsimonious MP. I think we should claim what we need to run our offices and pay our staff but be careful because it's obviously public money. In a year, rent for the office in Durham Road, Finsbury Park, is about £12,000 to £14,000."

He rents his office from the Ethical Property Company, who he described as "fine people".

"Hosanna to the Ethical Property people," he said raising his mug of coffee as a toast.

He was happy to described himself as "parsimonious".

"Well, I don't spend a lot of money," he said. "I lead a very normal life, I ride a bicycle and I don't have a car."

He was once the proud owner of a Ford Fiesta, but it kept on getting stolen. Once it was used as a getaway car in the robbery. On another occasion, he offered tea and cake on the Commons' terrace as a reward for its return. That was before he became concerned about air pollution. Accusing the government of overlooking the needs of public transport in 1992, he said: "There has to be a limit on the numbers of private motor cars in our cities. There is a limit to the amount of pollution we can go on tolerating."

However, all that cycling did not come cheap. MPs can claim 20p per mile. In 2007, he filed a claim for £230, which meant he had cycled an impressive 1,150 miles, topping the list for parliamentary cyclists.

"Jeremy is extremely hardworking, particularly as a constituency MP," Diane Abbott said. "He is an amazing constituency MP. He has his bicycle and cycles to see people. He does have other interests though. He adores his sons, he has three sons. And he loves his allotment. And he actually reads a lot. So he's not a one-dimensional figure. He's certainly not some sort of creature of the Labour Party machine."

For Corbyn cycling was not only a means of getting from place to place. He described it as "the summit of human endeavour ... the perfect marriage of technology and human endeavour". For longer journeys, he takes the train and, whenever he is late, always seizes the excuse to make a remark about renationalising the railways.

He also makes that point on board the train. According to Kevin McGuire, associate editor of the *Daily Mirror*: "He makes his sandwiches for long train journeys. I have spoken to people who say he shares the sandwiches. If you haven't got any he says don't bother going to the buffet car and spending your money on this privatized rail company. Here you are – don't contribute to their profits – have one of my sandwiches."

Chapter Ten – Return to the Wilderness

During the thirteen years of the Labour government, Corbyn had never ceased to be a trenchant critic of the government, so his position would change little with David Cameron in Number Ten. Yet again, in the election in 2010, Corbyn managed to increase his share of the vote in Islington North. He now sought to prove his credentials as a leftist intellectual with an erudite forward thinking approach to a new edition of J.A. Hobson's classic work *Imperialism*.

A man of principle, he did not shift his position, even when it caused outrage. In November 2012, he hosted a meeting at the House of Commons organized by the Palestine Solidarity Campaign where Mouss Abu Maria was invited to speak. Abu Maria has previously been convicted of membership of Palestinian Islamic Jihad, a banned terrorist organization under UK law. However, he claimed that he was no longer involved with the PIJ, but rather the Palestine Solidarity Project, an organization that said it was dedicated to opposing the Israeli occupation of Palestinian land through non-violent direct action.

The same year, Corbyn also agreed to speak alongside Muslim converts Abdurraheem Green, a presenter on Peace TV, and Wasim Kempson of the Islamic Channel, at a conference held at Arsenal

FC's Emirates stadium, his home turf. But the club barred Green from its premises at the last minute after it was alleged that he advocated a husband's right to beat his wife.

On the domestic front, there was austerity to fight. In February 2013, Corbyn joined Tony Benn, leading trades unionist, authors Tariq Ali and Iain Banks, journalist John Pilger, filmmaker Ken Loach, peace campaigner Bruce Kent, Lindsey German, convenor of the Stop the War Coalition, Richard Bagley, editor of the *Morning Star*, the leaders of the Communist Party of Britain and many others in signing a letter to the *Guardian* lending their support to the People's Assembly Against Austerity. This organization had been formed to fight for all those people they saw as being hit by government policies, including low-paid workers, disabled people, unemployed people, the young, black, minority and ethnic groups and women. The letter said:

"This is a call to all those millions of people in Britain who face an impoverished and uncertain year as their wages, jobs, conditions and welfare provision come under renewed attack by the government. With some 80 percent of austerity measures still to come, and with the government lengthening the time they expect cuts to last, we are calling a People's Assembly Against Austerity to bring together campaigns against cuts and privatisation with trade unionists in a movement for social justice. We aim to develop a strategy for resistance to mobilise millions of people against the Con Dem government.

"The assembly will provide a national forum for anti-austerity views which, while increasingly popular, are barely represented in parliament. A People's Assembly can play a key role in ensuring that this uncaring government faces a movement of opposition broad enough and powerful enough to generate successful co-ordinated action, including strike action. The assembly will be ready to support co-ordinated industrial action and national demonstrations against austerity, if possible synchronising with mobilisations across Europe. The People's Assembly Against Austerity will meet at Central Hall, Westminster, on 22 June (register at www.coalitionofresistance.org.uk)."

Later that month, Corbyn attended "The All-Encompassing Revolution" seminar at the Islamic Centre of England in Maida Vale, held to celebrate the thirty-fifth anniversary of the Islamic Revolution in Iran. He gave a talked called "The Case of Iran", calling for the immediate scrapping of sanctions on the country, attacked its colonial exploitation by British business and called for an end to its demonization by the West.

In 2013, Corbyn married Laura Alvarez in her native Mexico. Twenty years his junior, she runs a small business importing "true artisanal Mexican coffee" produced by small co-operatives in her homeland.

"The marriage is still going," said Piers. "She is committed to the cause and is active."

They shared their home with Italian journalist Gian Maria Volpicelli, who wrote in *L'Espresso* that Corbyn was not teetotal. In an article about Cobyn, he said that Corbyn had been compared to Albus Dumbledore, the headmaster of Hogwarts in the Harry Potter books. Corbyn said: "I do not like this comparision, it is a bit silly."

At the end of June he flew to Gaza with his wife and a researcher. There were complaints that their £2,821 trip was paid for by charity Interpal which the US has put on a sanctions list, claiming that it was "part of the funding network of Hamas". However, the UK Charity Commission has accepted that it has broken its connection with the Palestinian organization. Corbyn has made other trips and has met with the leadership of Hamas several times.

He has also spoken on platforms with representatives of the Lebanese party Hezbollah. Asked in an interview on Channel 4 News in July 2015 why he had called Hamas and Hezbollah "friends" at a parliamentary meeting, Corbyn explained that he had used the word in a "collective way", and does not condone the actions of either organization.

"There is not going to be a peace process unless there is talks involving Israel, Hezbollah and Hamas and I think everyone knows that," he argued. "I spoke at a meeting about the Middle East crisis in parliament and there were people there from Hezbollah and I said I welcomed our friends from Hezbollah to have a discussion and a debate, and I said I wanted Hamas to be part of that debate.

"I have met Hamas in Lebanon and I've met Hezbollah in this country and Lebanon. The wider question is Hamas and Hezbollah are part of a wider peace process. Even the former head of Mossad says that there has to be talks involving Hamas. I've also had discussions with people from the right in Israeli politics who have the same view possibly that the state of Israel should extend from the river to the sea, as it is claimed people from the Palestinian side do."

Corbyn is unrepentant.

"Yes, I've met [the Hamas leader] Khaled Meshal," he said. "I've met people from all these groups, actually, with a number of other people; Tony Blair has too."

After leaving office as prime minister, Blair was the United Nation Middle East peace envoy.

Diane Abbott rallied to Corbyn's defence.

"Jeremy campaigns for actually talking to the IRA, actually resolving the problems in Ireland. He was proved absolutely right," she said. "As to Hezbollah, all Jeremy is saying is that you have to talk to people. And to smear Jeremy by saying he's a friend of... no, he believes you should resolve things ideally politically."

However, his old mucker Leo McKintrisy said: "There's an almost childlike Marxist view that the West is always wrong. The British government's always wrong and any self-styled liberation movement is always right. He seems to have transferred his support from the Irish republicanism to Hezbollah because they fit this world view."

Despite the cynics' sneers about his poor choice of friends, Corbyn's efforts were recognized. In November 2013, Corbyn was awarded the Gandhi International Peace Award for his "consistent efforts over a thirty-year parliamentary career to uphold the Gandhian values of social justice and non-violence".

The Gandhi Foundation said: "Besides being a popular and hard-working constituency MP he has made time to speak and write extensively in support of human rights at home and world-wide. His committed opposition to neo-colonial wars and to nuclear weapons has repeatedly shown the lack of truth in the arguments of those who have opposed him."

He was ten minutes late for the award ceremony at Portcullis House because he had been attending the switching on of the Christmas lights in Newington Green, which had been postponed for half-an-hour. Then he had had to cycle to Westminster, though it was all down hill. Despite the prestigious occasion, Corbyn put his constituency first.

Accepting the award, Corbyn naturally praised Gandhi and committed himself to Gandhi's ideals. Conducting the ceremony was Jeremy's old friend from CND, Bruce Kent.

"His birthday is May 26, the same as St Eleutherius who was Pope in the second century," said Kent, a former Roman Catholic priest. "Jeremy is never going to be a Pope, but he could be a martyr. His school motto was 'serve and obey', which is one lesson he's never learned. I've never met a man who is so willing to be available to anybody at any time."

That year, Corbyn received the Grassroot Diplomat Initiative Honouree for his "ongoing support for a number of non-government organizations and civil causes". Grassroot Diplomat is a UK-based non-profit, non-political, diplomatic consultancy established in 2011 that aims to bridge the gap between governments and civil society. Its awards were designed to recognise outstanding diplomats and politicians who represent the people's interest at the highest level.

In January 2014, Corbyn visited Iran. This drew criticism because the trip was partly funded by Ardeshir Naghshineh, the Iranian-born head of a British property company that once owned London's Centre Point. However, also on the trip were former Labour Foreign Secretary Jack Straw, now consultant to ED&F Man, one of the world's biggest commodities traders, and former Conservative Chancellor Lord Lamont, then a consultant to Targetfollow and to the British-Iraqi billionaire Nadhmi Auchi, a key Middle East intermediary for the oil industry. Corbyn had no commercial ties.

In foreign policy, Corbyn remained staunchly anti-American. In April 2014, after the Russian Federation annex Crimea and pro-Russian militias armed themselves in eastern Ukraine, Corbyn pointed out that this was the result of the US's untrammelled march to the east.

"The expansion of Nato into Poland and the Czech Republic has particularly increased tensions with Russia," he wrote in the *Morning Star*. "Agreements Gorbachov reached before the final demise of the Soviet Union and subsequent pledges that Ukraine's independence would not see it brought into Nato or any other military alliance appear to have been forgotten…"

He did not condone Russia's behaviour or expansion, but said it was not unprovoked.

"The far-right is now sitting in government in Ukraine," he pointed out. "The EU and Nato have now become tools of US policy."

And he warned that a new cold war beckoned.

"Taken slightly historically, the turning point in the EU was actually the Single European Act, the Thatcher/Maastricht-era stuff, which was turning the EU into very much a market system," he said. "Setting up an independent European Central Bank, which then promotes the euro, and I think the sheer brutality of the way they've treated Greece, makes me question an awful lot. The other side of it is, I think, that Labour should be making demands about working arrangements across Europe, about levels of corporate taxation across Europe. There has to be agreement on environmental regulation… Why are we leaving it all to Cameron, to put together a statement, when he's had no negotiations with anybody?"

He was also concerned about the plight of Greece.

"Look at it another way: if we allow unaccountable forces to destroy an economy like Greece, when all that bailout money isn't going to the Greek people, it's going to various banks all across Europe, then I think we need to think very, very carefully about what role they [the EU] are playing and what role we are playing in that," he said.

Under Miliband, he kept up his opposition from the backbenches. During his career in parliament defied the whip 533 times, making him by far the most rebellious Labour MP.

In the 2015 election, Corbyn was one of sixteen signatories to an open letter to Ed Miliband calling for Labour to make a commitment to opposing further austerity, to take rail franchises back into public ownership, and to strengthen collective bargaining arrangements.

Over public spending, they rejected Labour's pledge to eliminate the current deficit by the end of the next parliament, calling for a £30 billion investment package funded either by higher borrowing, the state-owned banks, a new round of quantitative easing, or a special levy on the super-rich.

Rather than Labour's plan to allow not-for-profit firms to bid for rail franchises as they expire, the MPs demanded that contracts are automatically returned to public ownership. And they called for the promotion of collective bargaining and improved recognition for unions.

This was a shot across Ed Miliband's bows by Corbyn, Diane Abbott, Michael Meacher, and other stalwarts of the Socialist Campaign Group. In the *New Statesman* on 26 January, they spelled out their demands clearly:

1. An alternative to the continuation of austerity and spending cuts till 2019-20

All three main parties, tragically, seem to agree that deep spending cuts must continue to be made until the structural budget deficit is wiped out in 2019-20, even though wages have already fallen 8 percent in real terms, business investment is still below pre-crash levels, unemployment is still two million, the trade deficit in manufactured goods at over £100 billion is now the largest in modern history, and household debt is now over £2 trillion and still rising.

The Tories want to continue with these cuts because it gives them political cover to achieve their real objective which is to shrink the State and squeeze the public sector back to where it was in the 1930s.

It isn't even as though the deficit is being reduced by these savage cuts. Because the reduction in the government's tax revenues as a result of shrinking incomes exceed the spending cuts, the deficit (which is still nearly £100 billion) is likely to rise, not fall, in 2014–15 and in future years.

There is an alternative way out of endless austerity. We need public investment to kick start the economy out of faltering growth and to generate real job creation and rising incomes.

It can readily be funded. With interest rates at 0.5 percent, a £30 billion investment package can be financed for just £150 million a year, enough to create more than a million real jobs within 2-3 years. And even without any increase in public borrowing at all, the same sum could equally be funded either through the two banks which are already in public ownership, or through printing money (quantitative easing) to be used directly for industrial investment rather than for bond-buying by the banks as hitherto, or through taxing the ultra-rich by a special levy.

2. Returning rail franchises when expired to public ownership rather than subjecting them to competition

The essence of rail reform must be to reverse fragmentation, to reintegrate the system under public ownership, and to run it in the public interest. At present Britain has the highest fares in Europe. The additional costs of privatisation to public funds are estimated at more than £11 billion, or around £1.2 billion a year, so that the costs to the taxpayer are now three times as much as under British Rail.

Since 2010 rail fares have increased 25 percent, yet at the same time more than £200 million a year has been paid out in dividends to shareholders or overseas state-owned rail companies which now hold two-thirds of the current rail franchises. Over 80 percent of the public want the railways re-nationalised, which must include a significant proportion of Tories.

The most obvious and simplest way to achieve this is by letting the rail franchises expire and then taking them back into public ownership at no cost whatever to the taxpayer. To subject them to a public bidding competition with private bidders is not only wholly unnecessary but sends out the wrong signals, as though we're not confident of our own ideology. The Tories certainly didn't offer a competitive option when they forced through privatization!

Anyway, the franchise process, so far from being economic, encourages the gaming of wildly optimistic passenger number projections and this, combined with huge legal contract complexity which is bureaucratic and wasteful both in time and money (except for the lawyers and accountants), has led in the past to franchise failures and operating chaos, most notably on the East and West Coast lines. From past experience public ownership has consistently worked better, and we should not gratuitously throw obstacles in our own path in getting there.

3. The need for the restoration of collective bargaining and employment rights as a check against excessive corporate power

When the Thatcher government came to office in 1979, 82 percent of workers in the UK had their main terms and conditions determined by a union-negotiated collective agreement. The latest figures now show that the coverage is down to just 23 percent. One very significant result is that the share of national income going to salaries and wages has fallen dramatically from 65 percent in 1980 to 53 percent in 2012 – a loss to employees of some £180 billion!

This has happened partly from the collapse in trade union membership from 55 percent of the workforce in 1979 to 23 percent in 2012. But it has also happened partly as a result of the anti-trade union laws introduced in the 1980–90s and partly because the state has withdrawn support for collective bargaining as part of the free market ideology of de-regulation of all markets, including the labour market. It is somewhat ironic however that de-regulation of the labour market requires the tightest regulation of one of the key players in that market, the trade union movement.

An incoming Labour government should choose to enhance the role of trade unions because trade union rights are human rights, a trade union presence creates more just and equal workplaces, and trade union collective bargaining is more redistributive than statutory wage setting and will assist on the road from austerity. We should therefore actively promote sectoral collective bargaining and strengthen the rights of trade unions to recognition, and of their members to representation.

This could practically have been Jeremy Corbyn's manifesto when he stood the leadership election and clause one's anti-austerity strategy would soon be called Corbynomics.

While Labour lost the election, Corbyn was returned to parliament for the eighth time in 2015 with 29,659 votes – 60.2 percent of those cast.

Back in parliament for the new session, he called for a ban on the importation of foie gras into the United Kingdom, supporting Kate Hoey's early day motion saying: "That this House deplores the production of foie gras, considering it cruel and unnatural to force-feed geese until it causes internal damage; welcomes the UK's continued ban on domestic production of this foodstuff; commends India on last year becoming the first country in the world to ban the import of foie gras; and calls on the Government to follow this example in making the UK the next country to ban the import of this most unpleasant product."

He was also a sponsor of a motion opposing the Yulin Dog Meat Festival, an annual celebration around the summer solstice in Guangxi, China, where dog meat and lychees are eaten; an estimated 10,000–15,000 dogs are consumed in around ten days. The early day motion said: "That this House condemns the plans to go ahead with the Yulin Dog Meat Festival 2015 in Yulin, China; expresses deep concern at the cruel and inhumane manner in which dogs have been slaughtered in the past; notes the terrible conditions that dogs face prior to being killed as they are held in overcrowded cages without water; and urges the Chinese authorities to intercede to stop the festival from taking place."

Clearly he is very particular when it comes to food. According to the *Financial Times*: "He loves making jam with fruit grown on his allotment, belongs to the All Party Parliamentary Group for Cheese and is a borderline trainspotter." The newspaper added that the only blue thing he professes affection for is a ripe Stilton.

Although such issues do have their place in politics, they hardly address the main question – which direction should the Labour Party take if it was ever to win power again.

Chapter Eleven – Jez We Can

Following Labour's defeat in the election 2015, Ed Miliband resigned. The deputy leader Harriet Harman took over as acting leader and a leadership election was called. Corbyn declared his candidacy immediately, telling the *Islington Tribune* that he would be standing in the election on a "clear anti-austerity platform". Corbyn added: "This decision is in response to an overwhelming call by Labour Party members who want to see a broader range of candidates and a thorough debate about the future of the party. I am standing to give Labour Party members a voice in this debate."

It soon became clear that Corbyn would struggle to secure the thirty-five nominations from the Parliamentary Labour Party required to enter the ballot before the deadline at noon on 15 June. However, several MPs were persuaded to nominate him, even though they did not intend to vote for him and he passed the threshold with two minutes to spare. He was still at the back of the field.

Andy Burnham topped the list with sixty-eight nominations, followed by Yvette Cooper on fifty-nine, Liz Kendall on forty-one and Jeremy Corbyn on thirty-six. However, after a series of TV and radio debates, Corbyn went on to gain the support of the UK's two largest trade unions, Unite and UNISON, and received the highest number of supporting nominations from Constituency Labour Parties. Soon he was ahead in the polls and at the bookmakers.

The party grandees rounded on him. Tony Blair told people who said their heart was with Corbyn: "Get a transplant." Alastair Campbell called for ABC – "Anyone But Corbyn".

The press attacked him with the *Sunday Times* saying that far from being parsimonious he had "jetted across the world at the taxpayer's expense". However, in *The Sun on Sunday*, Boris Johnson said of Corbyn: "These days you look at what is happening in Iraq and Syria – the almost daily bombings and massacres – and you have to respect his judgment."

Support came from other unexpected quarters. Users of the popular parenting site Mumsnet found him "sexy" – which Corbyn said was "the most embarrassing thing" he "ever heard". More than £100,000 in donations poured into his campaign via crowdfunding. Labour Party membership soared by over a quarter of a million and young people greeted Corbyn everywhere with the chant: "Jez we can."

"We have changed the debate within the party," he said. "In a sense, we have already won."

Then on 12 September 2015, Jeremy Corbyn was elected Leader of the Labour Party, with a landslide vote of 59.5 per cent in the first round of the ballot. This was larger than Tony Blair's lead in 1994. Corbyn's nearest rival, Andy Burnham, was 40 per cent behind with just 19 per cent of the vote. Yvette Cooper got 17 per cent, while Liz Kendall polled 4.5 per cent. This silenced critics who claimed that Corbyn had been unfairly favoured by new rules that allowed anyone who paid a £3 registration fee could take part in the vote. There were rumours that numerous Conservatives had joined up to vote for Corbyn, who was seen as a liability for Labour in any general election. However, the party said there were procedures in place to weed out those would did not "support the aims and values of the Labour Party" – which, in themselves, caused controversy.

After the result of the leadership election was announced, Corbyn's first act was to attend a "refugees welcome here" rally, joining tens of thousands of people marching through central London in support of the rights of refugees. Addressing cheering crowds in Parliament Square, he delivered an impassioned plea to the government to recognize its legal obligations to refugees from Syria and elsewhere and to find "peaceful solutions to the world's problems".

The following Wednesday he donned a new suit to attended the weekly Prime Minister's Questions in the House of Common, one of the great parliamentary set pieces. Traditionally, this involves sparring between the prime minister and the leader of the opposition. Corbyn took it in a new direction. He did not ask his own questions, or those written for him by his staff. Instead he selected questions solicited from the public – six picked from the forty thousand emails he said he had received.

Praise for this innovation was lost among the welter of criticism over his failure to sing the national anthem at a service at St Paul's Cathedral the day before marking the seven-fifth anniversary of the Battle of Britain. An ardent anti-monarchist, he could not bring himself to sing "God Save the Queen". However, he promised to sing it in future and agreed to become a member of the Privy Council – the cabal of senior politicians who serve as the Queen's closest advisors. The induction ceremony traditionally involves kneeling before the monarch. In the end, he did not kneel. However, he did kiss her hand.

He was also criticized for not giving top jobs in his shadow cabinet to women, but rather to his chums on the hard left. However, the gender balance was maintained in his shadow cabinet team as a whole. One of his most vociferous supporters throughout these tribulations was Diane Abbott who he made Shadow Secretary of State for International Development. The press then had a field day when they discovered that they had been lovers during his break-up with his first wife.

Abbott, then a young civil-rights campaign, hopped on the back of Corbyn's bike for a romantic tour of Communist East Germany and, in an interview Abbott gave to *She* magazine in 1985 when she was running to be Labour's parliamentary candidate in Brent East, she described a naked romp with a man in a field in the Cotswolds as her "finest half-hour". The man concerned was, she said, a "long-time friend and very close" ally, though she refused to name names.

Party activists already knew of the liaison. Corbyn had shown off his new love by inviting canvassers back to his bedsit on the pretext that he had left some leaflets there. They found to their evident surprise a naked Diane on a mattress on the floor with the duvet pulled up to her neck.

Corbyn's first wife, Jane Chapman, then told the *Mail on Sunday* of a confrontation with Abbott a few months after she had left her husband. She had moved into a one-bedroom flat above a jeweller's shop in Crouch End, North London, when suddenly Abbott turned up on her doorstep. It was "quite a shock," said Chapman.

Abbott was "nervous, tense and slightly hostile". Nevertheless, Chapman invited her in and they had a short and unpleasant exchange.

"She wasn't very nice when she called on me, but I'm not going to go into that," said Chapman. "She told me to get out of town. That was basically how the conversation went. But I was still a councillor. I had been elected for years and that hadn't expired, so I still had responsibilities. And I was still going to meetings and Jeremy and I were still seeing each other there."

Abbott, she concluded, was jealous. At the time, Chapman had not known that Abbott had replaced her on Jeremy's pillion.

Westminster wags quickly dubbed him the "Sexpot trot", but remained baffled by his unfathomable attraction for women. Corbyn it seemed had succeeded in overturning another of the great traditions of British politics – that scandals in the Labour Party concern money, while sex is left to the Tories. The affair lasted a year.

Chapter Twelve – The PLP versus the Party

After being a long-time rebel against the front bench, Corbyn found it hard to command the loyalty of the Parliamentary Labour Party. When Prime Minister David Cameron set out the case for airstrikes on Syria as part of a strategy to defeat ISIS, following their attack in Paris that November, Shadow Foreign Secretary Hilary Benn supported intervention, while Corbyn was against it. He was then forced to give Labour members a free vote on the issue. Sixty-six Labour MPS, including Benn and Deputy Leader Tom Watson voted with the government, while Corbyn and 152 other Labour members voted against. The motion was carried by 397 votes against 223. Nevertheless in the January reshuffle, Benn and Watson retained their positions in the Shadow Cabinet. Meanwhile, a number of junior shadow ministers resigned over other sackings and party infighting.

Benn and Corbyn were still sitting shoulder to shoulder when they met US President Barack Obama on his visit to London in April. After discussing "the challenges facing post-industrial societies and the power of global corporations and the increasing use of technology around the world and the effect that has", Obama went on to play golf with the prime minister.

In the House of Commons, Cameron's personal attacks on Corbyn reached a new low when a Labour MP asked David Cameron what his mother would say about the state of the National Health Service as she had signed a petition opposing cuts to children's centres.

Directing his reply at the Leader of the Opposition, Cameron said: "Ask my mother? I think I know what my mother would say. I think she'd look across the dispatch box and she'd say: put on a proper suit, do up your tie and sing the national anthem."

Corbyn immediately hit back, citing his late mother, Naomi, who had been a peace campaigner.

"Talking of motherly advice," he said, "my late mother would have said: 'stand up for the principle of a health service free at the point of use' because that is what she dedicated her life to, as did many people of her generation."

When the EU Referendum was called, Corbyn said that the Labour Party would back Remain. The case for staying in was overwhelming as the EU protected workers' rights. However, he had voted for coming out in the 1975 referendum, had opposed the Maastricht and Lisbon treaties, and backed the call for a referendum in 2011. Even in July 2015, he said he was ready to join the Leave campaign if Cameron traded away workers' rights, environmental protection and failed to crack down on Brussels-backed tax havens. Then, the morning after the vote, Corbyn called for the prime minister to trigger article 50, beginning the withdraw process, immediately.

Remainers blamed Corbyn's lukewarm support for their loss, though Diane Abbott and others rallied to his support, pointing out that he had campaigned tirelessly, though with little coverate. But the Parliamentary Labour Party were soon in open rebellion. Corbyn had to sack Benn for trying to organize a mass resignation of the shadow cabinet to force him to stand down. A torrent of other resignations follow as Corbyn lost more than two-thirds of his shadow cabinet. He tried to staunch the flow, appointing new members to fill the gaps. Some refused posts, while Pat Glass, newly appointed Shadow Education Secretary, quit after two days saying the situation was untenable.

On 27 June, Corbyn lost a vote of no confidence by Labour MPs by 172 to 40. But he insisted that he had been elected by an overwhelm majority of the party as a whole only nine months before. The confidence vote did not automatically trigger a leadership election, he said, and he refused to quit.

"I was democratically elected leader of our party for a new kind of politics by sixty per cent of Labour members and supporters, and I will not betray them by resigning," he said. "Today's vote by MPs has no constitutional legitimacy."

The problem was that Labour was consuming itself in internal fighting when it should have been capitalizing on the Tories' disarray following the resignation of David Cameron. However, during the outgoing prime minister's last appearance in the House of Commons, Corbyn landed a couple of blows.

"I'd also like you to pass on my thanks to your mum for her advice about ties and suits and songs," he said. "It's extremely kind of her and I'd be grateful if you could pass that on to her personally. I'm reflecting on the lesson she offered."

Then he added: "But I've got one rumour I want you to deal with. There's a rumour going around that your departure has been carefully choreographed so you can slip seamlessly into the vacancy created this morning on *Strictly* by Len Goodman's departure. Is that your next career?"

But Corbyn's difficulties were still behind him – the PLP and their repeated attempts to oust him. Union leaders and the redoubtable Diane Abbot, now Shadow Health Secretary, once more rallied to Corbyn's defence. She said that, if there was another leadership election, she thought he would win.

One of the faultlines in the Labour Party has always been nuclear weapons. Facing a debate on the renewal of the Trident system, Corbyn suggested that the UK should have new Trident submarines, but not carrying nuclear missiles. This would protect jobs in the defence industries while fulfilling his lifelong commitment to unilateral nuclear disarmament. However, other members of the PLP were not prepared to live with the compromise and he was forced to give the party a free vote again.

In the House, the new Prime Minister Theresa May said that she would authorize a nuclear strike, if required, even though she would then be responsible for the deaths of hundreds of thousands of people. But Corbyn made it plain that he would not press the nuclear button.

"I make it clear today I would not take a decision that kills millions of innocent people," he told MPs. "I do not believe the threat of mass murder is a legitimate way to deal with international relations."

Some 140 Labour MPs voted for the renewal of Trident, while forty-seven joined Corbyn in voting against. Another forty-one were absent or abstained.

By then, a leadership contest was underway. After she had resigned as Shadow First Secretary of State, Angela Eagle, who voted to renew Trident, launched a leadership challenge. The question then arose whether Corbyn would need to secure the required number of nominations to run or would he have the automatic right to stand as incumbent leader. The National Executive Committee decided that he did. When challenged, this decision was upheld in the High Court.

The NEC also decided that only those who had joined the party before 12 January 2016 had the right to vote. That meant the 130,000 who had joined since the EU Referendum were ineligible. This issue was resolved when the ballot was extended to "registered supporters" who paid £25 in the forty-eight hours before 5 pm on 20 July; 183,541 did, raising £4,588,525 for the party.

The former Shadow Secretary of State for Work and Pensions in Corbyn's first shadow cabinet Owen Smith then stood for the leadership, saying that Corbyn was "not a leader who can lead us into an election and win for Labour". Smith quickly outdistanced Angela Eagle in the race for nominations and she pulled out, fearing that if they both ran it would split the anti-Corbyn vote.

While Corbyn slumped against Theresa May in opinion polls taken among the general public, among Labour supporters Corbyn was streets ahead of Smith. Since he had first run for the leadership, membership of the party has soared to over half a million, more than all the other parties put together.

Nevertheless, Corbyn is consistently ridiculed by the newspapers. On 11 August, he was filmed sitting on the floor of the London to Newcastle express, claiming that the train was "ram-packed" and he could not find a seat. Virgin boss Richard Branson then released CCTV footage of Corbyn walking passed empty seats. Jeremy later explained that single seat would not suffice. He had needed to sit with his wife and his team to prepare for his meeting in Newcastle. He then turned down an upgrade to first class, but was found a seat when a sympathetic manager upgraded other passengers to make room in the standard compartment.

While the newspapers scoffed, Corbyn succeeded in highlighting the plight of ordinary rail users, fed up with overcrowded trains. Sixty per cent of passengers now back renationalization of the railways.

This was quickly forgotten as the leadership hustings came to a close. The result was announced on 24 September at the beginning of the Labour Party Conference in Liverpool. In a vote of other half-a-million party membership, he increased his support, this time wining 61.8 per cent of the vote. He took 313,209 votes against Smith's 193,229, even though his first wife, Jane Chapman, public announced that she had changed her mind and this time she would vote against her ex-husband.

Smith conceded with a handshake, though he had previously announced that he would not serve in Corbyn's shadow cabinet.

"Jeremy has won the contest," he said. "He now has to win the country and he will have my support in trying to do so."

Corbyn then extended an olive branch. In his victory speech, he said: "We have much more in common than divides us. Let us wipe that slate clean from today and get on with the work that we have to do as a party together."

He went on to make a triumphant appearance at The World Transformed festival, organized by Momentum, the grassroots group that has been closely involved in his campaign, where he was greeted by cheering supports. It was clear that Jeremy now had a mandate to take the Labour Party in a new, radical direction.

Printed in Great Britain
by Amazon